#266

D1131283

FRESCO PAINTING

FRESCO PAINTING

Modern Methods and Techniques for Painting in Fresco and Secco

by

OLLE NORDMARK

AMERICAN ARTISTS GROUP, INC.

NEW YORK

FRESCO PAINTING

COPYRIGHT, 1947, BY
AMERICAN ARTISTS GROUP, INC.

All rights reserved, including the right to reproduce this book or portions thereof in any form.

PRINTED IN THE UNITED STATES OF AMERICA

PREFACE

This book has been written for the painter in fresco, who wishes to acquire enough knowledge of the craft to enable him to supervise, guide and efficiently work with the craftsmen plasterers who are put in charge of the preparation of his materials and wall and who will assist him as the finishing plasterers throughout the period of painting.

It should be remembered that the surface of the so-called "Intonaco," must yield the best possible working conditions, giving the painter the longest possible time to execute the part of the wall intended for a day's work. In order that such a condition should prevail, a thorough knowledge of the materials used in the practice of fresco painting must be acquired through the practical utilization of a series of operations to obtain necessary ultimate results.

Stress is, therefore, laid upon the fact that the painter himself must guide and guard the preparation of his materials and the different layers of mortar which build up the fresco ground, the foundation for the painting. Also, if he is not prepared himself to do the work, he must be able to give final full directions for the "Intonaco" or painting surface, the richness of the mixing and its perfect application which in itself requires experienced handling of tools in the piece-meal plastering of the wall, all of which is the groundwork for the actual painting.

This HANDBOOK, therefore, will endeavor to explain the practice of fresco and fresco-secco painting in connection and collaboration with the trade from which it was derived — the building trade.

OLLE NORDMARK

CONTENTS

COLOR PLATES

FRESCO PAINTING

WALLS

THE QUESTION of a suitable wall for the fresco-mural, or how to make any available area a permanent foundation for the plaster coats making up the fresco ground, has vexed the fresco painter from ancient times to our days.

BRICK WALLS

Generally it can be said that the old-fashioned brick wall made from handmade bricks is still the ideal wall for the fresco-mural. Bricks baked to a fresh looking red and laid in lime-sand mortar constitute that kind of a wall.

Old plastered walls must first have the plaster removed. Old as well as new walls are cleaned with a weak solution of HYDROCHLORIC ACID, washed with hot water and then sprayed and rinsed with cold.

During the spraying the wall is examined for non-absorbent bricks of a muddy violet or clincer grey color. All such bricks baked and burnt beyond the temperature of the fresh red color must either be insulated by waterproofing or, better still, replaced with good bricks to remove the ever present possibility of EFFLORESCENCE. Waterproofing is done by painting over with an ASPHALT type of WATERPROOFING which will still allow the mortar to cling to the safeguarded brick.

Deep hollows and faulty bricks are filled out and repaired with lime-sand mortar, 1-2 mixture with brick chips mixed in

3

as a filler. All the brick joints are raked back about 1/4" and smooth bricks roughened with a stone cutter's hammer made for the purpose.

HOLLOWTILE WALLS

The next best wall will unquestionably be the hollowtile wall; the tiles set with the flutes in checkerboard pattern or interwalls of horizontally running flutes, thus "checking" in all directions. Tiles deeply grooved or dovetailed are the best for a good plaster bond.

Tile walls laid in Portland cement mixed brick mortar, such walls have if old and dry partition walls, only the mortar joints waterproofed. Walls backing the outside are given an allover waterproofing and "furred out." The waterproofing is done twice to insure against air bubbles bursting under the brush and leaving small wide open pin holes.

The dead air space in tile walls remove much of the danger of efflorescence, the whitish exudation seen on old walls and especially on outside brick chimneys. The wall is examined in the same way as the brick wall for non-absorbent tiles and for necessary repairs. The abundance of grooves makes raking back of the joints or roughening superfluous.

FURRING WALLS

"Furring Out," means setting off a new wall in front of one already built. This provides for dead air space the extra protection of the surface of the "furred out" wall. The waterproofing of the building wall and the air space left between is a good guarantee against destruction due to moisture. Furred out panels can be employed by the fresco painter to great advantage giving him a practical and perfectly safe wall to work on if certain precautions are taken to ensure a stable and strong surface.

4

As described previously the building wall is first cleaned and waterproofed.

Second, FURRING STRIPS are nailed to the wall, spaced according to the width of the metal lath, and given a coat of waterproofing. (*See illustration.*)

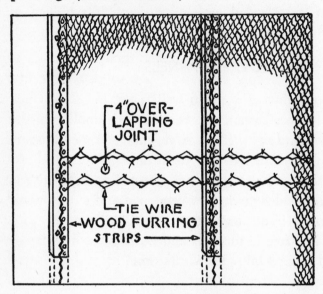

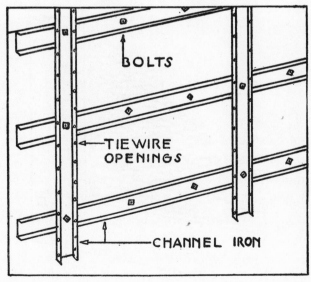

Furring strips are usually made of pine, perfectly dry and straight to avoid warping followed by cracking of the plaster. Large size fresco-murals call for a more extensive furring job. Galvanized channel iron strips are employed, fastened to the wall with EXPANSION BOLTS and screws. Still larger murals would have to be provided with expansion joints hidden in the picture composition.

MOVABLE PANELS

Another possibility of a fresco wall is the movable panel, practical only up to a certain size because of crumbling of the edges from its own weight. If too large, they become unwieldy especially panels constructed with steel frames.

More practical and also easier and cheaper to make are the panels built on wooden frames. A very rigid and strong panel can be built on a frame made from kiln dried pine or hard birch, straight and free from knots and water-proofed with two coats of boiled linseed oil. (See *illustration*.)

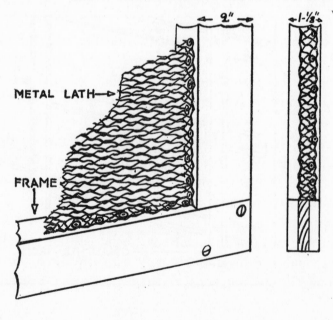

6

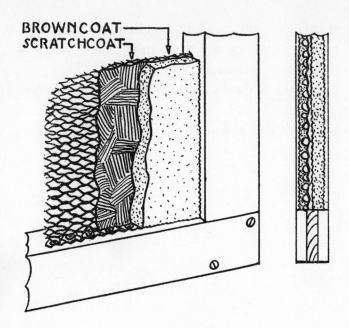

BROWNCOAT
SCRATCHCOAT

FURRING

The next step in furring is the nailing of METAL LATH on the furring strips, using galvanized roofing nails with large flat heads.

Of the many kinds of metal lath available, only the heavy, twisted, galvanized lath is good enough for a permanent wall. Incidentally the author remembers having painted secco on walls, sand finished over split reeds woven into lengths of mats with anniled wire and nailed onto the studding. This type of wall was widely used before the advent of the metal lath and a big improvement on the old wooden lath strips. In spite of the age, such walls are still in perfect shape, thanks to the lime-sand plaster coatings and surfacing by "floating," a term explained later.

The free edges of the nailed on metal lath are overlapped about 4″ and tied together securely with galvanized tie wire. Mere tying by spacing ties 6″ apart as in common practice is

7

not good enough. Only by lacing together and tying both over-lapped edges can the metal lath be made into a taut and rigid base for the fresco ground.

In conclusion, it should be remembered that partition walls are the very safest. Walls backing the outside must receive an allover waterproofing and be furred out as well.

PREPARATION OF MORTAR MATERIALS

CHAPTER TWO

LIME

ONLY THE HIGH CALCIUM LIME is used in the preparation of mortar for fresco painting. It is sold in bulk and called LUMP-LIME or POWDERED LIME in containers or paper bags.

The lumplime is fairly hard to work with. In the slaking process the pieces or the lumps pop and the big ones may get too hot before they can be quenched that they burn and lose their effectiveness in mortar altogether. Also, if slaked by inexperienced help, it might prove to be dangerous.

Powdered lime can be slaked with less work and without fear of being spoiled by burning if only ordinary care is taken, such as slaking only a small amount at a time and thus controlling the process. After slaking, the lime will readily settle and form a viscous LIME PUTTY which should be stored in a tight box or steel drum or better still, in a lime pit. Best of all slaked limes is the so-called lime putty, matured for more than a year, put up and shipped in steel drums. HOT LIME and QUICK LIME are other names for unslaked lime.

Hydrated lime can be dismissed right here as worthless for fresco painting. Like most of the cheaper limes it contains magnesia which takes years to slake and small amounts continue to slake years after it has dried. The familiar sight of cracking, bulging and falling chunks of plaster is most often caused by magnesia in the lime. Another dangerous impurity

9

is gypsum, of which, even a small percentage cannot be tolerated.

The best lime is pure-white, an important factor in fresco painting because of its transparency and its ability of bleaching to a snowy white, the reflecting surface under the colors.

Remember, that lime is a transparent product that appears opaque when freshly painted out and rather dull looking at first. After having dried and hardened for over a year, the painting, because of the lime's bleaching ability, becomes drawn together in tonality, with beautifully transparent depths and clear lustre in the lights. Years of continued carbonization will gradually give depth and richness in tone to the colors.

LIME SLAKING

The most practical arrangement for lime slaking is to have two boxes built, one over the other. The upper box is pitched slightly forward and provided with a run-off gate opening into the lower box. (*See illustration.*) Slaking takes place in the

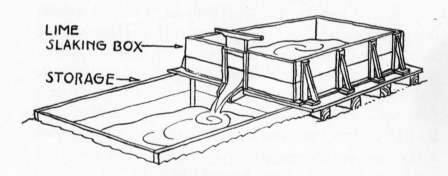

LIME
SLAKING BOX

STORAGE

upper box and the lime is let out from time to time by running it through the gate into the lower box to leave room for slaking and to cool off before storage.

The slaking is simple. A water-hose is hung over the edge of the box and the flow regulated to a slow stream. Fill in the lime a little at a time, hoeing and mixing lime and water and watching for hot dry piles that must be quickly quenched before they are burnt by drying and overheating. Slake at the upper end of the box and hoe down toward the gate. The box is emptied into the lower one and when sufficiently cooled off, the lime is stored in a PIT or in STEEL DRUMS provided with a tight cover and rubber packing. The storage space may be any cool dark room or cellar.

Steel drums, painted on the inside with asphalt varnish or baked lacquer, are used for storing lime and mortar.

All empty bags should be disposed of to keep unslaked lime from settling on other materials.

Lime to be aged for a year or two is better stored in a pit. A square hole is dug in the ground and the bottom filled to a depth of three or four inches with sand or gravel upon which the flooring is laid. A similar space is also left around the sides and filled in with gravel. This will act as drainage and help keep the pit dry on the outside.

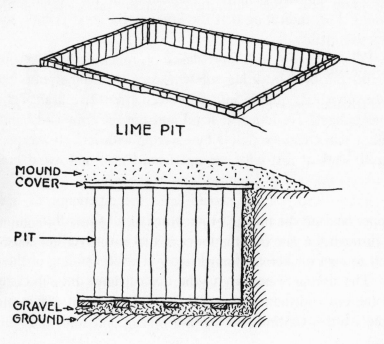

LIME PIT

MOUND→
COVER→

PIT→

GRAVEL→
GROUND→

Before putting the lime into the pit, it should have had a chance to cool off in the box. Hot lime may cause the boards to warp and open up. It is also advisable to add extra water to the lime before closing the pit. Water kept standing over the lime as long as possible will considerably increase thorough slaking by prolonging the process. A heavy and tight cover made of tongue and grove boards like the lining, is nailed down and covered with sand or gravel. Finally the earth is shoveled back covering the whole. The pit must be deep and well covered up over the winter to keep the lime from freezing. Once frozen it is completely spoiled.

Before purchasing lime for fresco work it would be advisable to test a small amount first under actual painting conditions. Slake and allow to mature for two weeks then mix an intonaco, two parts lime and five parts fine sand, and paint a full scale detail on a small panel. A good lime sets up in nine hours time and the colors should then withstand spraying with a water hose. The intonaco should not come clean off the trowel; some should cling, indicating that the lime is of a good viscous and adhesive quality.

When working with lime, slaked or unslaked, avoid getting it into the eyes by using safety glasses. Hot lime from the slaking box eats quickly into unprotected sensitive flesh. Have a neutralizing eye lotion at hand and protect arms and hands with a skin cream or simply by covering with lard. If inexperienced, work at first with an experienced man and avoid lime burns on the skin and spoiled lime in the box.

Every fresco painter should have the experience of lime slaking and mortar mixing, work which at all times throughout the painting, is the guiding principle that can never be ignored in fresco work. Ultimate knowledge and understanding of these two materials are necessary to the fresco painter for successful mural work. Freedom in painting comes from knowing and being able to control the materials.

SAND

Sand and lime are the only two components in the fresco mortar as a rule, but in certain cases crushed tile or white stainless cement is added to the scratch coat.

The sand varies a little but only two kinds are used in fresco, either BANKSAND or MARBLE MEAL and MARBLE DUST. The coarser meal is used in the ground and the so-called dust in the intonaco. CRUSHED QUARTZ would be a valuable addition except for its excessive sharpness which will rub off steel from the trowel and make the surface spotty and grey.

Banksand is preferred by some fresco painters for the warm colortone it gives to the painting. Others use the whiter marble dust and paint a suitable surface tone as required.

Banksand is selected from dry and clean pits. It must be of a uniform grit, free from loam, clay, gypsum, etc., and should

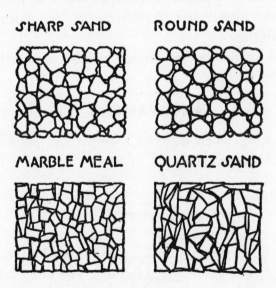

SHARP SAND   ROUND SAND

MARBLE MEAL   QUARTZ SAND

contain a high percentage of quartz, feel sharp and not roll between the fingers. The idea of using sharp sand is to squeeze the mortar tight and this is possible in plastering only when the sand is made up of small wedgelike particles, packed tightly together and leaving the smallest possible space for the lime when mixed into mortar.

Round sand rolls under the trowel and will not stay squeezed down. The large spaces between the grains of sand will, when mixed with lime, make the mortar loose and crumbly.

Sand that contains MICA (small transparent flakes easily split and divided), is unsuitable for fresco work. Mica on the intonaco surface and painted over, will sooner or later split, divide and fall off, leaving a white spot.

Loam or gypsum, present in the sand, might develop the familiar ugly spots of efflorescence, while clay makes the mortar loose.

Clean handling of sand, washed or unwashed, is essential and best done by bagging the sand in new tight BURLAP BAGS. Beware of old cement bags and keep the sand from touching the ground. Sand, bricks and tile, heaped direct on the ground, pick up all the ingredients of efflorescence, the death of any lime color painting.

All this fuss and bother cannot be dispensed-with if the final work, the painting, is valued at all.

SAND WASHING

Sand washing, when done in a simple and practical way, need not frighten anyone.

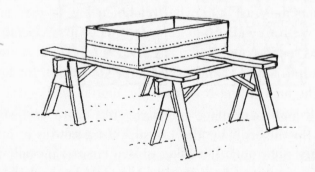

A couple of HORSES, two SCREENS of different mesh, a large DRYING PLATFORM raised a foot from the ground and a WATER-HOSE comprise the sand washing equipment. The screens are fitted one on top of the other and are of the same size. The lower screen is made of 28-34 mesh, reinforced with galvanized metal lath underneath, and the upper screen is equipped with window fly screen or 16 per inch mesh.

A shovelful of sand is dumped into the upper screen, played over with the hose and raked back and forth with a piece of hardwood until the fine sand has washed through the upper screen leaving only the rough. The rough sand is dumped off at one end of the platform and the fine sand in the lower screen

DRYING PLATFORM

is now washed in the same manner as before, "blowsand" and mud landing below on the ground. The fine sand in the lower screen is now dumped off at the opposite end and the piles are raked out in even distribution on the platform. To speed up the drying, the sand is furrowed with the corner of the hoe, first in one direction and when commencing to dry, in the opposite. Re-furrowing from time to time will accelerate the process. As soon as one section has dried out the sand is immediately put into a bag to allow space on the platform for further drying. The final sifting is done in the mortar box.

Marble meal and marble dust is washed and handled like the sand. Crushed tile does not need to be washed.

The first and rough screening is used in scratch coats where the sand is combined with crushed tile. The finer, in the sand finish and in intonaco. From time to time during the washing, a handful of washed sand is thrown into a glass of clear water. Clean sand sinks to the bottom, leaving the water clear; muddy water and floatings on the surface indicate unsatisfactory washing. Muddy shoes should not be worn when walking over the sand and a roll of roofing paper should be at hand to cover up the platform with lengths of paper over laid boards in case of rain. Also, cover everything up tight each night after work to keep out animals. Once, in Oklahoma, a skunk visited the author's drying platform and two day's work had to be thrown out.

Cleanliness is the A.B.C. of fresco work. One's own hands, the tools and materials as well as the room where the work is done should be kept clean at all times. Free lime dust, allowed to settle on sand and colors can do a great deal of damage that is not easily detected at first.

MORTAR MIXING

CHAPTER THREE

SUCCESS IN FRESCO PAINTING depends entirely upon proper handling of the mortar materials both before and after they are mixed together.

Sand must be kept dry and not touch the ground. Lime must be kept from freezing and drying out in the pit or the box. Re-mixing the mortar several times before it is used will help to insure a successful conclusion of the work.

Only clean and dry sand, together with high calcium lime in putty form, makes good mortar. Wet or damp sand will not make a workable mixture, neither will watery lime. The wet surface of the stone particles making up the sand will keep the lime from carbonizing and adhering directly onto that surface. The space, however microscopic, formed between the particles is accountable for the failure of the plaster coat. Because of the lack of adhesiveness such mortar does not work well under the trowel or the float.

Tight and homogeneous unification of the sand with the lime is essential to coherence in plaster coats.

TOOLS AND EQUIPMENT

Like most of the tools and equipment for fresco work, the tools needed for mortar work are few and simple. A MIXING BOX, lime PUDDLE BOX, a couple of MIXING HOES, three galvanized BUCKETS, a STEEL BARREL for water, two SHOVELS and a WHEEL BARROW complete the list.

The mixing box is always made from new lumber. It must be built strong, large and tight and provided with a tight cover. (*See illustration.*)

MIXING BOX

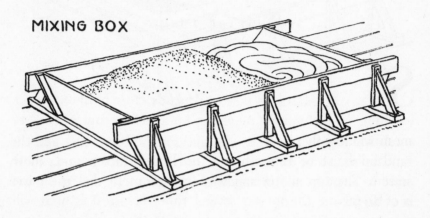

Old boxes, scaled from old lime or mortar and boxes that were used for gypsum plaster should not be used for fresco mortar. They can never be so completely cleaned that the danger of efflorescence will be eliminated.

Long handled large mixing hoes, the kind with two round openings, are the most efficient.

The water barrel is kept close to the box within handy reach for rinsing and cleaning tools to prevent mortar from collecting and hardening on the tool surfaces, making them unfit for the work.

All tools and the mixing box are thoroughly wetted down before being used. Many uses will be found for the wheelbarrow around the job. Use vaseline on the hands and wear cotton gloves when working with mortar and, if inexperienced, safety glasses should be worn.

Sifting of the sand is the first step in mortar mixing.

Two boards or battens are placed across the box to support the sandsift. For sifting heavy sands, used in grounds, a 14-16

18

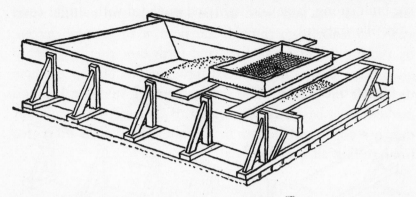

mesh window fly screen is used and for the browncoat and the sand finish, 18 or 20 mesh and for the intonaco a 32-34 mesh screen. The top sift in sandwashing, 18 mesh and the lower is of 29-30.

SAND SIFT

SUPPORTING METAL LATH

BRONZE MESH

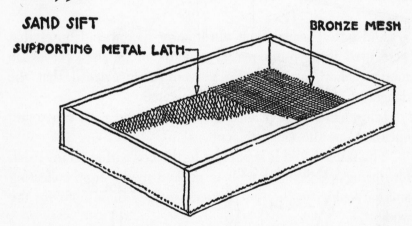

A level bucket of sand is poured into the sift and shaken through. For every bucket of sand sifted into the box, a grease pencil stroke is made on the outside of the box thus keeping close count of the intended mixture. Always measure in buckets for shovelsful are too irregular. Extra buckets are counted in for sifting waste.

After the correct amount of sand has been sifted into the box the lime is added. The simplest way of squeezing lime

19

through a sieve is to use a PUDDLE BOX. (*See illustration.*) The lime is first cut and hoed in the lime box and a little water added to make it go through the sieve, a 29-32 mesh screen. By rocking the PUDDLER back and forth over the lime even a quite heavy putty can be forced through. The heavier the lime the better the mortar. The lime is counted into the box and marked down beside the sandcount. By placing the puddle box over a scooped out hollow in the sand the lime is prevented from getting all over the box.

LIME PUDDLING

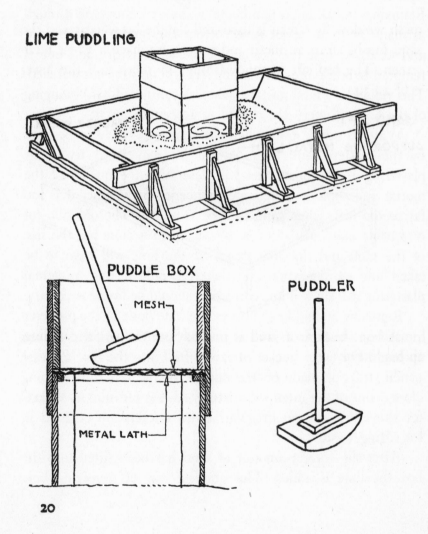

PUDDLE BOX

MESH

METAL LATH

PUDDLER

After measuring the materials correctly, they are mixed together with the hoe and shoveled to one end of the box in a heap. If the box is big, two men, each with a hoe, can work side by side CHOPPING, slicing and cutting the mortar down to the opposite end of the box. The chopping is continued until the batch has been worked over twice. No more water should be added at this time. The cover is placed over the box and the mortar is left to "soak" for two days. This preliminary soaking is a time and work saving device and increases the toughness of the mortar. It will also make it easier to work with. Remixing, the all important chore, is done by chopping through as many as six or seven times before the mortar is taken out and used. At first the mortar looks and feels dry and one is tempted to add more water; choppers will do so if not watched. This would be a fatal mistake, whereas continued hard swinging of the hoe will merit the reward of a perfect mortar.

Water is added only when the mortar is ready to be used by the plasterer and then only at his request. A tryout by plastering a few square feet will determine the quality of the mortar and show if more water is needed or whether it is too fat or too lean when sand or lime is added. The old rule for measuring materials; 1-3, 1-2, 5-7, or 50-50 is close but the size of the sand and the consistency of the lime will have to be taken into consideration and therefore only testing by actual plastering will show if any correction should be found necessary.

Remixing and adding of water is always done by the plasterer himself on the table as well as the quick remixing before filling up his "hawk".

PLASTERING THE FRESCO GROUND

CHAPTER FOUR

To give the uninitiated an idea of how plastering is done it is best to begin by describing the tools. (See *illustrations*.)

The PLASTERER'S TABLE is his working table upon which he remixes the batch for final uniformity, using additional water, and working up the mortar until ready to be laid over the wall. Only fine mortar is worked up on the table, rough mortar for grounds is thrown from a small box. The plasterer's helper brings the mortar from the box in buckets and places it on the table.

PLASTERERS TABLE

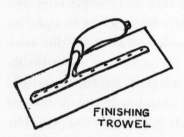

FINISHING
TROWEL

The FINISHING TROWEL, an exceedingly important tool in plastering, must be made of the finest possible steel, light and flexible with a long aluminum handle riveted to the blade with ten rivets and a hardwood handle with a curved sweep. It should be perfectly straight and faultless, without nicks or rust eaten spots. An especially smooth and shiny trowel is reserved for intonaco plastering. Two other kinds of trowels are also used

22

by the plasterer; a diamond shaped, broad, MIXING TROWEL and a small diamond shaped POINTING TROWEL used for cleaning up bigger tools and for "pointing up" in intonaco plastering.

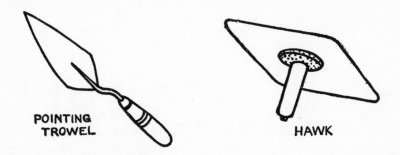

POINTING
TROWEL

HAWK

The HAWK is the plasterer's palette, a square piece of aluminum with a hardwood handle in the middle cushioned with a sponge rubber ring around the handle underneath the square.

The hawk is held in the left hand while carrying a load of plaster from the table. A couple of strokes with the trowel cleans off the edges of the hawk and the work is ready to begin. The edge of the hawk is held against the wall and the plasterer lifts from it a trowel full of mortar which he squeezes straight up and down again on the wall. Stroke by stroke until the hawk is empty, the mortar is laid on as far as he can conveniently reach upwards and sideways. The hawk is loaded again and the work proceeds until an area of convenient size is covered which can be quickly straightened and made smooth. The mortar should be spread sideways and squeezed down to an even thickness and the surface made smooth by vertical and horizontal strokes of the trowel, gliding first on one edge, then on the other coming back. The hawk is quickly filled again and the work proceeds horizontally from top to bottom the complete length of the wall. Large areas require several plasterers standing in a row to keep the edge of the mortar from setting before the adjoining section is spread on.

23

LEVELING

The leveling of the wall is done before the plastering can take place. The WATER LEVEL and a six foot long STRAIGHTEDGE constitute the equipment. The following quick and simple method is widely used by the trade.

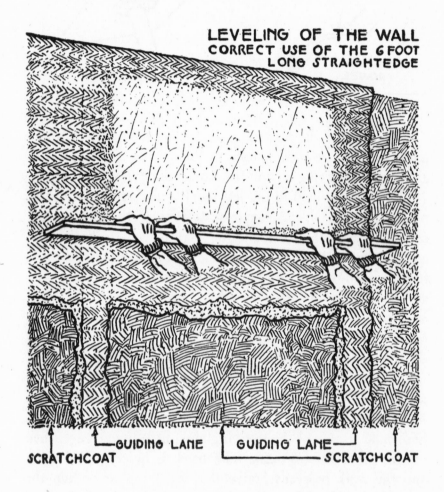

LEVELING OF THE WALL
CORRECT USE OF THE 6 FOOT
LONG STRAIGHTEDGE

GUIDING LANE | GUIDING LANE
SCRATCHCOAT | SCRATCHCOAT

In a corner of the wall, a vertical lane of mortar, the width of the trowel, is spread on and five feet away from this lane another one. Along the top edge, a third lane is plastered between the two preceeding ones. The edge of the straightedge board is set down along and on top of the lane and by moving the board up and down, is rubbed across the plaster. Holding the waterlevel against the other edge of the board the level will show if the lanes are plumb and straight. The lane at the top is also straightened, by rubbing the straightedge from the bottom to the top, guided by the vertical lanes.

Plastering is continued between the lanes without destroying the level. Using the lanes as guides, the straightedge is rubbed horizontally from bottom, upwards to the top, hollows filled in and rubbed off until the whole plastered area is even with the guiding lanes. The surface is tried with the straightedge and the water level, and if not found satisfactory, mortar is applied again where needed and rubbed off as before until straight. Mortar accumulated on the straightedge is cleaned by thumping against the boards laid out under the working area alongside the wall to catch the surplus mortar falling during the plastering. If perfectly clean the mortar is scooped up from the boards and mixed into the batch.

By using plumb lanes for guides, area after area can be quickly plastered straight, leveling off from the preceeding correct area to the last laid up lane, throughout the length of the wall. If a lower part is going to be joined, the upper finished one of course serves as the guide.

The herringbone pattern markings, caused by rubbing the straightedge over the surface, are left, if deep enough, to serve as a scratch coat. Otherwise the wall is scratched with a comb made for the purpose.

There is a common belief among plasterers that one can scratch with anything that makes a mark and in any old way. This is a mistake as marking a surface is one thing and making a scratch coat is an entirely different thing.

SCRATCH COAT

From a piece of galvanized sheet iron a COMB with long teeth is cut out. (*See illustration.*) This type of comb will scratch deep without loosening the mortar. Combing in all directions will evenly distribute the "hooks" (protrusions of sand particles, ridges, etc.), and prevent uneven suction; this is important in fresco work. Very meticulous scratch coating, is to my experience the best insurance against complications during and after the work is finished.

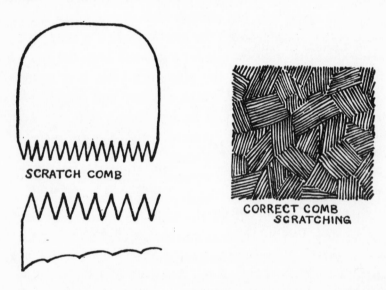

SCRATCH COMB

CORRECT COMB
SCRATCHING

Over a well wetted down brick wall an ordinary sand-lime coat, mixed from 1 part lime and $2\frac{1}{2}$ to 3 parts of sand is laid on to a thickness of about $\frac{1}{4}''$. This coating is scratched with the comb and before it is left to set it is given a fine spray of water.

Over smooth brick and hollow tile walls this type of scratch coat is also thrown, (spattered on as in cases of hard-burnt surfaces). Spattering or throwing of the scratch coats has been the common practice in Europe since mediaeval times especially in barrel and ribceilings, the sand finish there, is still thrown with a broad trowel, mortar throwing is a skillfully performed operation much admired by the author in his youth.

Before describing the next mortar layer the so-called "brown-coat," another type of scratch coat will have to be thoroughly investigated since this mortar coat is laid over metal lath.

SCRATCH COAT WITH STAINLESS WHITE CEMENT

The mortar used for this kind of work is mixed from 1 part lime and 2 to 2½ parts sand. To prevent the mortar from falling through the metal lath, just enough fiber or goat's hair is mixed in. The fiber is sprinkled over the mortar while it is being mixed. Soaking the goat's hair in lime for a day will burn out fats, etc. When the mortar reaches the plasterer's table it is sprinkled over with ATLAS STAINLESS WHITE CEMENT and quickly mixed together. The amount should be less than 1/5th the mortar volume. The purpose of the cement is to make the metal lath rigid and it is used only in the scratch coat.

The quick setting of the cement precludes the pre-mixing and therefore the plasterer must rely on his experience for accurate measurement. With the finishing trowel, the mortar is spread over the metal lath as quickly as possible. Immediately after, before the surface has become too hard, deep and vigorous scratching is done, holding the comb in a slanting position, thus making sharp and slightly inverted grooves in the surface. The hooks, sharp and tough, will give the following coat a secure grip.

To set the cement hard and homogeneously in the plaster coat, prolonged spraying with water for two or three days and covering with a wet sheet is of the utmost importance. This serves the same purpose as the wet hay on a newly poured concrete road.

The dry scratch coated metal lath should not yield to the pressure of the hand. The mortar that has squeezed through the openings and locked itself on the back, is called the "key", and if broken, the stability of the whole ground is lost. In case the key is broken, spraying with water and the laying of a second scratch coat a trifle fatter in lime and cement should take care of such a mishap.

Over all places where the metal lath is doubled up and tied, special care is taken to "key in" the overlapping edges.

The "browncoat" or "browning" is the trade name for the next layer of mortar over the scratch coat. The different layers of mortar in a ground differ most in their methods of application.

BROWNCOAT

The browncoat is made a little fatter by using less sand, 1 part lime and $2\frac{1}{2}$ parts of sand. Before beginning the plastering of the browncoat, the surface is wetted down hard with a fine spray, with short intervals of rest to allow the water to draw back and to soak in. In order to facilitate continuous work before advanced setting has taken place in the mortar, laying of so-called SKIMCOAT will greatly help to slow up the setting. Advantageous, in time-consuming operations like leveling and floating. The skimcoat is a part of the browning mortar thinned out with more water, quickly and thinly spread over the undercoating. Skimcoats will effectively retard setting and prolong the working time. Another advantage is that by dividing the plastering into two operations a much heavier layer can safely be laid on. Laying of the full thickness at once would only invite trouble. The skimcoat will also hinder the formation of air bubbles and pockets in the mortar during the plastering.

After a short time of setting the browncoat is laid over the skimcoat and finished by checking and pressing back air bubbles, cracks, etc. Again, all over scratching with the comb completes the browncoat.

28

SANDFINISH

Sandfinish is a term applied to a sand-lime mortar coat where the surface is finished by FLOATS (tools common to the plastering trade). Although varied and made from many kinds of

SANDFINISHING
SHINGLE FLOAT

materials, to suit particular types of work, fresco painters are concerned only with one kind, the float made from an untreated ROOF SHINGLE, selected from tight and straight grained boards. HARDWOOD HANDLES are made or bought to fit different sizes and fastened with a couple of screws to the shingle board. When the board is worn thin it must be replaced or at first the screws can be turned below the surface to permit further use of the float. To keep the floats from warping, they are placed in a bucket of water and weighted down. New float boards are sandpapered smooth for very fine plastering finishes. The underedges of the shingle are rounded and tapered off slightly to keep the edge from cutting into the surface. The finely balanced distribution of lime and suction in sandfinish is the work of a good float, the pleasant sweep of the shingle board and its lightness will soon be felt and understood by anyone who has had a chance to float a piece of sandfinish.

Plasterers not familiar with sand-lime mortar plastering will undoubtedly recommend the floats of their experience, such as the carpet, cork and felt floats. They are good when used for gypsum plastering but entirely useless for fresco work if not outrightly destructive. The absorbent covering will, when not too wet, pull the lime out to the surface and settle it there in spots and streaks. Also when an absorbent float is dipped in water or slides over a water spattered area, it becomes filled up and will wash out the surface lime completely. This uneven distribution of lime results in some spots becoming stone hard, others washed out and too absorbent and the surface worn and troubled looking like a badly grounded canvas. Therefore, selection of the right kind of a float should be given special attention by the painter.

FLOATING

Only after a whole wall or panel is finished and troweled smooth and as soon as the surface can stand the pressure of the fingers does the floating begin. At the beginning, little or no water is spattered on, probably just an occasional dipping of the float is enough. Sandfinish or floated surfacing is done as follows:—A plasterer's wetting brush is held in the left hand

WETTING
BRUSH

a bucket of clear water kept nearby. The brush is dipped into the bucket and the water is spattered over the surface to be floated. The float is also dipped into the water and rubbed over the plaster with a firm pressure and circular movements. If the plaster is still tender the pressure is very light at first. The floating begins at the end where it was first laid on. Just ahead of the float, the water is spattered with the brush in uniform co-ordination with the float, slightly cutting and distributing the mortar evenly. No other paint surface than the expertly troweled or floated lime-sand surface has the same soft lustrous texture and silvery tone.

CRACKS will sometimes appear in the mortar when plastering over uneven walls with deep hollows. In themselves such cracks are not dangerous if they develop immediately after the plastering. They can quickly be remedied by brushing over a little thin watery lime, pushed back and squeezed together with the trowel. Scratching over the spot will prevent the cracks from reappearing.

Checking the plaster coat for solidity after it has dried out, is simply done by tapping the surface with the wooden end of a pencil or any similar piece of wood. The hollow sound will tell if the plaster coat is loose in any place and by marking off the spot the plaster can be pulled out and replaced.

ADDITIONAL SUGGESTIONS

Rough mortar hangs on in thicker coating than finer mixings.

Fine mortar will fall off, if laid on too thick, because of its own weight. 1/5th of an inch seems to be the limit for thickness.

Combing the surface of a rough mortar such as one combined with an aggregate of crushed tile is superfluous.

The ground scratch coat, laid directly on the wall, should be left to dry completely before it is followed up with overlaid coats. The key position of this coat makes careful checking by tapping the surface and correction of the faults doubly important.

When smoothing the mortar with the finishing trowel, small air bubbles may develop in the mortar over deep places and in deep plaster coats. By puncturing the air bubbles with a needle or the corner of the trowel and pressing them out, they will disappear without further trouble.

FRESCO GROUNDS

CHAPTER FIVE

Fresco grounds are generally divided into 3-4 layers of mortar. The first layer, called the "scratchcoat" is the coarsest and the leanest of the layers. The following one is called the "browncoat," made of finer sand and slightly fatter. The third layer, the "sand finish," is rubbed "floated" into the nearly dry browncoat. The last coat, the "intonaco" or painting coat is laid piecemeal over the ground.

Only two kinds of fresco grounds are necessary for lime painting. The sand and lime ground is sometimes made with a filler of crushed tile in the scratch coat. Marble meal and marble dust are the components of the second kind. The first ground can be used for any kind of intonaco—fine sand intonaco or the highly finished marble dust surface.

A good ground must have depth, if too shallow, the ground does not hold the moisture long enough to develop the heavy "skin" of carbonized lime which is the protective sealer of the colors.

Trying to make up for a poor ground by painting over a thick and fat intonaco layer is a common mistake made by inexperienced painters. Complete ruin by efflorescence and darkening, flattening out of the values by graying will soon follow. Small pinholes, observed on the painted surface, lack of depth in the dark color areas, and the general troubled appearance of the tonality have all originated from the same source, the shallowness of the ground. Depth in color values comes from good lime, a deep ground and rapid painting sessions.

The ground of today, with some small variations, is very much the same as the one described by the Roman architect Vitruvius. He speaks about the "trullisatio," the first and roughest coat, corresponding to our scratch coat, the "arricciato" and the "arenato," the second two coats very similar to our browncoat and sand finish and finally the "intonaco" or the uppermost coat which receives the painting. Hereafter, for the sake of clearness and expediency the Italian name *intonaco* will be used for the last coating.

Ancient practice still holds good; a lean rough mortar laid straight on the wall, followed by the other coats, fatter and finer, and the intonaco, the finest and richest, acting as a sealer for the ground and the color surface.

Successful grounds for fresco and secco painting should not measure under 1¼″ in depth. Ancient grounds often measured not less than 3″ and some as much as 4″ in depth. Where a highly finished surface is desired, only a ground between 1¾″ to 2″ will properly support the intonaco throughout the prolonged troweling such a finish requires.

The old "gesso" ground laid over a wood panel and the fresco ground are both derived from the same principle:—lean-rough to fat-fine. The "gesso grosso" is the same as the scratch coat, "gesso sotili" the browncoat and the last burnished and polished surfacing would be synonymous with the intonaco.

The grounds made up from lime and sand with CRUSHED TILE introduced into the scratch coat are of ancient tradition and well adapted to brick or hollow tile walls.

LIME AND SAND GROUND

Coarse sand washed in the upper screen is sifted through a 12 mesh sift and dry mixed with little more than a third

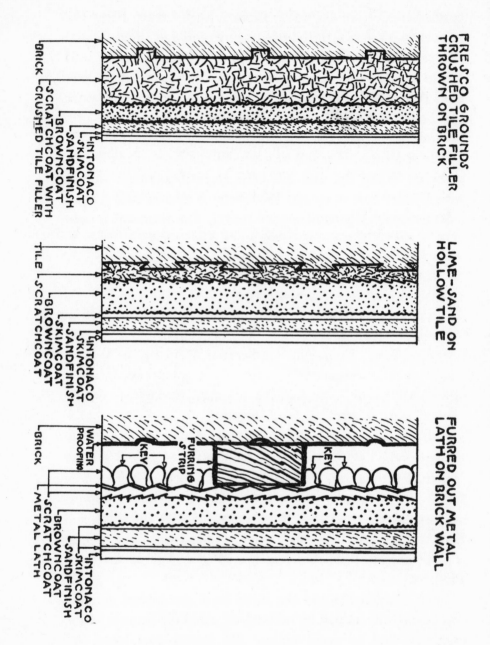

FRESCO GROUNDS
CRUSHED TILE FILLER
THROWN ON BRICK

BRICK
SCRATCHCOAT WITH
CRUSHED TILE FILLER
BROWNCOAT
SANDFINISH
SKIMCOAT
INTONACO

LIME-SAND ON
HOLLOW TILE

TILE
SCRATCHCOAT
BROWNCOAT
SANDFINISH
SKIMCOAT
INTONACO

FURRED OUT METAL
LATH ON BRICK WALL

BRICK
WATER PROOFING
KEY
FURRING STRIP
KEY
METAL LATH
SCRATCHCOAT
BROWNCOAT
SANDFINISH
SKIMCOAT
INTONACO

34

crushed tiles or pottery waste. Broken, unglazed red burnt tiles or pottery is crushed to the size of split peas and sifted through a larger than 12 mesh sift and well dry mixed with the sand. 2½ to 3 parts of the dry mixture is mixed with 1 part of puddled lime. After soaking for two days, without the addition of water, the batch is remixed several times by chopping until of a uniform color. After the first two choppings, the water is added, a little at a time, so as not to wash out the lime from the sand particles. When the wall has been given a thorough wetting with a water hose or sprayer the mortar is thrown with a squat looking, broad, diamond shaped trowel. The throwing is done

MORTAR THROWING
TROWEL

a short distance from the wall and in a slanting direction, from the left to the right, with a slight twist of the trowel for a wider spatter of the mortar. Surplus mortar, falling in the process of throwing, is retrieved from new boards laid out underneath as catchers. Mortar thus picked up is remixed with the batch and thrown again until the first layer is spread out. The mortar is thrown from a smaller box moved alongside as the work advances.

The straightedge and the water level are applied and the coat is carefully leveled by rubbing off; carefully because of the roughness and to avoid pulling the mortar coat loose. Air bubbles and pockets do not develop in a thrown mortar coat. The throwing is done sideways, as otherwise too much of the mortar is apt to bounce off the wall. Thrown rough mortar clings in thickness close to $\frac{1}{2}$" or more, depending upon the porosity of the wall. This first layer is left to dry and after good spraying with water, another equally thick coat of the same mortar is thrown and leveled as before. As soon as permissible, a brown coat, 1 part lime and $2\frac{1}{4}$ parts sand is plastered over the rough undercoating. The browncoat should be about $\frac{1}{4}$" to $\frac{1}{2}$" thick and scratched. When this coat in turn has become hard enough to work over, the sand finish is applied, made up of 1 lime and 2 sand, divided into a skimcoat, laid first and followed immediately by a second layer, floated as described earlier.

The lime sand ground can be used without the inclusion of the pottery filler. However, such a ground cannot hold the same amount of moisture necessary for deep carbonization as the ground made partly from a filler. The lean nature and toughness of this ground makes it valuable for two reasons, its greater ability to hold moisture longer, promoting faster and deeper carbonization, and prolongation of the painting period.

MARBLEMEAL GROUND

Grounds made from MARBLEMEAL and MARBLE DUST are especially adapted for the highly finished and lustrous marble dust intonaco.

Coarse marblemeal grounds (see *illustration*) are mixed from 1 part lime and $2\frac{1}{2}$ parts coarse marblemeal, 12" mesh sifting. On the mixing table, immediately before it is spread, 1/5 part of ATLAS stainless white cement is sprinkled over and mixed into the batch. Fiber or goat's hair is also added if used over metal lath. Cement mixed coatings are always kept wet for days in order to set the cement before the mortar has dried. Only in this way is it safe to use the cement in the key mortar coat.

On brick and hollow tile walls with a good porosity, a thin scratch coat, mixed as described above without the cement, is spattered or thrown over the wall and left to dry out. The coat is sprayed thoroughly with water and soaked before the second or browncoat, mixed from 1 part lime and 2 parts marblemeal, finer than in the scratchcoat, is applied. This coat is also scratched as usual with the comb. Before the second coat has hardened or as soon as it is possible to work over it without breaking the layer, apply the sand finish, 1 part lime and 2 parts marble dust. This is also divided into two operations, first a skimcoat is laid as usual and shortly after, a thicker coat is floated on as described previously. Thus the fresco ground is gradually built up of layers from coarse to fine, from lean to fat.

INTONACO

CHAPTER SIX

"INTONACO" is the old Italian name applied to the last mortar layer upon which the painting is made. The question of what kind of surface finishing the intonaco should have is more or less subject to the personal taste of the painter and the character of his painting. Some prefer transparency and smoothness in their work and desire the intonaco troweled to a fine finish. Others might prefer the floated finish with a slight tooth. Each should be tried on a testing panel for suitability.

Painting over a highly finished intonaco takes skill as the suggested smoothness brings out every stroke, good or bad. The difficulty of control of color tones is met by the use of the smaller size water color brushes and the scenic painters "fitches," brushes with long soft bristles.

Skillful handling of the FINISHING TROWEL and the ability of plastering piecemeal, repeating and equalizing every part of the work are the requirements of marble dust plastering. Intonaco of this kind calls for real skill and experience to attain the shiny burnished looking finish.

To succeed in getting this smooth finish a fault free trowel of the best quality, perfectly straight and with the edges worn down to a round thinness, is needed. Plasterers use such a trowel first in sand finishing until the edges are worn down smooth and round, but without the trowel losing its shape. Burnishing with No. 000 emery paper gives an additional smoothness to the blade. Together with his brushes, the finishing trowel is the fresco painter's most important tool.

The diamond shaped POINTING TROWEL of equally fine quality, flexible and smothe, is the second tool used in intonaco work. Smaller shapes from the mould maker's trade should be selected for detail work. Very useful is the one with a square edge at one end and a pointed, slightly bent one at the other. For cutting into plaster a moulder's knifelike tool, of a different shape at each end, is good.

Finishing trowels must never be put down with the blade flat on the table. Placed in this way they develop rust spots quickly, making them useless for fine work. Cleaned in water and wiped dry, they are left resting on the edge by themselves on a new piece of wooden board. Dropped, they will crack easily or if carried together with heavier tools, they will not keep their true shape. Mortar, if not carefully cleaned off, will collect and harden on a trowel until it becomes almost impossible to remove. Scraping and sandpapering, not hammering, is the remedy.

INTONACO PLASTERING

A new table top, replacing the one used for the coarser mortar, is placed on the stand and wetted down. The intonaco is remixed until uniform in color and water added. Tools are inspected for possible coarse sand particles still clinging to them as one particle of sand will mar the surface in many places.

Because of the slow setting of tight and fine intonaco, the work should begin early in the morning. An early start, at 6 or 7, for the plasterer is generally the rule. Careful handling and prolonged troweling and sometimes a long wait for the surface to settle down will cut the time limit for painting considerably. The slow and careful painting of the first color tones over the tender surface will also take more than it's fair share of the time allotted for painting.

Intonaco plastering is divided into two operations. First, a thin watery skim coat is laid and floated, cutting into the hardened undercoating. This will take care of the limeskin and condition the surface for the next layer. The best practice is to lay another thin coat over the skim coat and wait for $\frac{1}{2}$ hour or so before the laying of the final part of the intonaco is begun. Slow building up of the last mortar coat is an insurance against too fast drying and setting. Furthermore it will promote heavier carbonization of the color layers.

MARBLE DUST INTONACO MIXING AND PLASTERING

Mixing intonaco is done in the same way as the other mortar mixing. Dry marble dust is sifted through a 34 mesh, or finer sift. As mentioned in the earlier description of the mortar, only a painting test will determine the fineness of the intonaco. The sifted marble dust is mixed with, if used on a sand ground, about 5 parts of lime and 7 parts of marble dust. On the marble-meal ground the intonaco requires more lime, up to 50-50 mixture depending upon the behavior of the ground in a painting test on a movable panel made from left over ground material.

The intonaco, preceded by a floated skim coat, is laid after the surface has been given a fine spray of fresh water. Full strength of intonaco is laid in an even thickness, about $\frac{1}{8}''$, (the thickness always less than $\frac{1}{4}''$). Dipped in a nearby bucket of fresh clean water the trowel is slowly run over in a slightly tilted position. At first the pressure is very light, hardly more than touching the mortar. Lime, pressed out, is wiped off the blade with a wet sponge, then rinsed in a second bucket and finally wiped dry by a couple of strokes against the overalls.

Dipping and running the trowel wet, will be necessary when hardening of the intonaco is felt. At the end, when the surface is nearly finished, the sweeps of the trowel are made in one direction. In case of a mishap (cutting into the surface, etc.), the uppermost layer, the intonaco, is scraped off altogether and a new piece is laid on. A fresh start is better than an attempt to patch, which would be a mistake, and would show later as a dark area of different texture in the finished painting.

Because the moisture in the mortar always leaves at the top first, troweling starts at the top and ends at the bottom where moisture will linger for a longer time. The appearance of grey spots and smudges on the surface is caused by rubbing off steel from the trowel, especially on quartz and marble dust. Lack of speed and skillful handling of the trowel or the inability of keeping ahead of the hardening of the mortar is most often responsible for grinding off the steel.

Usually under prolonged troweling, air bubbles form in the intonaco, rarely when the skim coat is used. A sewing needle driven into a wood handle, is used to prick the air bubbles, after which they are pressed back in the troweling process.

SAND INTONACO

Intonaco made up from finely sifted banksand (about 7 parts to 5 parts of lime), similar to the sand ground, is less susceptible to changes causing cracks and color surface injury. Because of the slight "tooth" left by the float the colors become imbedded below the surface between the sand particles. Yielding a heavier carbonization over the colors, such a surface will become exceedingly tough and impervious to injury after a few years of hardening and deep carbonization. Handling and float-

SMALL INTONACO
FLOATS

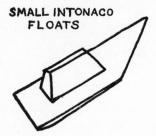
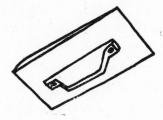

ing is the same as the sand finish. Floats of various sizes and shapes are used. (See *illustrations*.)

As a matter of personal taste this intonaco is used either floated alone or only given a surfacing with a few light strokes of the trowel. After a light spray of water and a rest to allow the water to draw back, the intonaco is ready for the transfer of the drawing.

Some fresco painters have eagerly looked around for something that will retard the setting of the lime in fresco-mortar. BUTANOL was one of the mediums tried. It is foreign to the nature of lime painting, especially fresco, to be loaded with detail and much admired brush work. Quite the opposite, fresco calls for simplicity and understanding of the limitations of the medium. To force the fresco medium to yield more time for painting, by use of a retarder, is to wish for an entirely different medium for self expression.

PRELIMINARY WORK TO PAINTING THE FRESCO

CHAPTER SEVEN

PAINTERS who are accustomed to preparing their own tempera or gouache colors from powdered pigments, will find no difficulty in doing so when preparing colors for fresco work. Understanding the technique involved in the piecemeal execution of the painting, will also present no difficulty if the painter is willing to prepare himself by getting familiar with the work as a whole. By assisting the plasterers, he soon will know how to do his own intonaco work and in a pinch, be able to lay in the area for that day's painting session himself.

This is only one example of getting oneself ready and prepared for the kind of work where the limited time for execution is its biggest drawback. Not only should the painter take the advantage of making himself familiar with the material and actual plastering, he should also have his own testing panels, at least three of them, for practising intonaco work and painting in the quiet of his studio. (More later about practising panels). The outcome of a painting in any technique depends entirely upon how prepared the painter is to do that particular painting.

COLORSKETCH

COLORSKETCHES are painted in tempera on light canvas on a stretcher and should be as large as can conveniently be carried around on a scaffolding. In the tempera, the color powders contemplated for the fresco should of course be employed in the painting of the sketch. This will start the painter off in the right direction and limit the tones to colors that are possible in fresco painting.

CARTOON

Detail in the colorsketch is of little or no value as all detail is worked out in the drawing of the CARTOON, the full size drawing of the whole composition from the colorsketch. Very

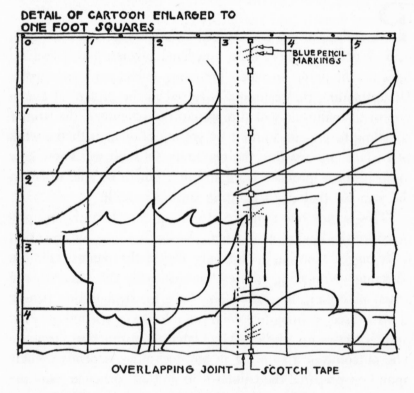

DETAIL OF CARTOON ENLARGED TO ONE FOOT SQUARES

OVERLAPPING JOINT — SCOTCH TAPE

strong detail paper or wrapping paper, in widths of 52″ to 72″ and of a light grey tone is the best kind. A TRACING of the sketch is made and squared up in proportion to the one-foot squares on the actual wall. Lengths of paper are cut, equal to the height of the fresco ground and hung plumb on the wall used for the

44

drawing work. Water level or plumbline is employed at the edge of each length of paper, tacked at the top and overlapped about three inches by the edge of the length. All paper lengths are hung loosely and the edges temporarily fastened together by widely spaced small pieces of SCOTCH TAPE. The squared up tracing is now enlarged within the limits of the ground marked on the cartoon papers. From the top down and from the left to the right side, using the waterlevel and the plumbline (the "snap line" in this case) the cartoon is squared up in 1 ft. squares and numbered, beginning with zero at the top left corner to the right and down the left side. Exactly the same system of numbering is copied on the tracing squares and must tally exactly with the cartoon. (See *illustration*.) If a toned paper of the same color as the wet intonaco can be found and the drawing is done in charcoal and highlighted very simply with white chalk the painter will have a realistic impression of the initial color values right from the beginning and from the very start avoid painting the values too light, thus sparing himself a lot of overpainting.

All edges of the finished cartoon are marked with short blue pencil lines running over the edge of each paper so as to enable the cartoon to be fitted together at any time.

TRACING PAPER lengths are hung over the cartoon and the squares as well as the drawing are traced with careful exactness, numbered as exactly as the cartoon and the sketch and also blue pencil-marked for fitting the lengths together when the tracings are used for transfer of the drawing to the intonaco.

45

Not enough can be said about the importance of accurate cartoons and tracings. The whole painting rests upon dependable tracings from accurate measurements on the cartoon. Inaccuracy will jeopardize the outcome of the whole fresco. The same accuracy is followed in the PERFORATING OF THE TRACINGS as well as the blue pencil-markings, turning them into POUNCES.

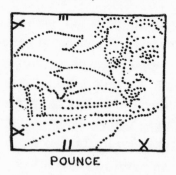

POUNCE

The tracing is laid out on a large table. Underneath the tracing is placed an old blanket folded double to save the points of the PERFORATING WHEEL and to keep the paper from tearing.

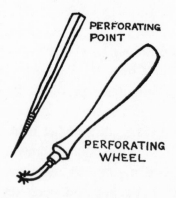

PERFORATING POINT

PERFORATING WHEEL

Only straight lines and large forms are perforated with the wheel. Faces, hands and anatomy in general are perforated by hand, using a SEWING NEEDLE mounted in a piece of wood for a handle. The needle works more like a pencil over a sensitive

46

drawing. The lines left by the wheel are apt to become very stereotyped and over small detail the wheel does not work very well. A fine SANDPAPER, used over the back of the pounce, will keep the openings of the perforation from closing when contacting the moist surface of the intonaco.

POUNCING

Pouncing is done by rubbing over the perforated lines with a ball filled with powdered charcoal. A double folded square of strong LINEN, fairly closely woven, is laid out and filled with the CHARCOAL POWDER. By lifting the edges together a ball is formed and a strong cord is wound around the edges several times and tied into a handle of the material completing the POUNCING BAG. Several sizes of pouncing bags are needed to do the dusting and kept in reserve in case a bag is punctured.

POUNCING
BAG

Careful dusting on the lines prevents the charcoal from flying over the intonaco and a circular movement of the bag will keep the pounce in place. In artificial light, or in side light from a window, transfer of unperforated drawings can be made by pressing off the lines in the soft intonaco. Any rounded BONEPOINT that leaves a fine line and does not tear the paper or scratch the surface can be used for making the imprint though only a strong tracing paper can stand the pressure of the point.

A perforating wheel with a swivel and widely spaced points should be selected. Close pointed wheels cause the perforated lines to open up and fall apart. Besides the waterlevel, the SNAPLINE is important as a drawing tool. Professional, non-twist snaplines are bought in hardware stores and a length, sufficient for the work, is wound up on a piece of wood. (See *illustration*.)

SNAPLINE WITH
PLUMB BOB

A small plumb bob tied to the loose end of the line will serve instead of the waterlevel on vertical lines. "Chalking" the line is done by rubbing it with broken pieces of charcoal sticks. Use of colors on the snaplines and in the pounce bag might result in serious smudging of the intonaco. Before snapping the line to transfer the charcoal, the line is lifted and let down gently again to loosen it from paper creases and rough mortar surfaces.

INTONACO PLASTERING, JOINING AND PAINTING THE FRESCO

The step by step method of explanation has been used for the sake of simplification in describing the painting part of this book.

A visual and graphic description will be helpful at the beginning of the painter's own tryouts and experiments on a movable test panel. The method will enable him to do his own intonaco plastering and joining of the areas, plastered piecemeal, work he should be able to do himself in case of necessity. After a series of plastering tryouts and detail painting in full scale, of parts considered to be of importance in the actual mural, he will, in a very short time, have gained the confidence and experience necessary for the work itself.

In large murals where big forms, such as houses or landscape lines, take up considerable space in the picture, construction lines of the forms should be drawn over the sand finish before intonaco plastering takes place. In this way the mural can be viewed as a whole. The drawing must be done in charcoal only, and the accumulated coal dust should be dusted off before the plastering. Slapping a flexible straightedge against the lines will do the dusting off and prevent the coal dust from being rubbed into the surface.

PIECEMEAL PLASTERING

Step 1—Wet the wall several times, from the bottom upwards, by using a water filled glass held against the surface and moved horizontally, allowing the water to flow down. Commencing at the bottom of the piece to be plastered and working horizontally upwards an effective soaking is accomplished and all loose dust washed off. Use the wetting brush in inconvenient places, corners, mouldings, etc.

Step 2—Mark off the area to be plastered with charcoal well beyond the actual piece intended for painting by leaving a margin of intonaco seven inches wide or more. The measurements should be made from the first pounce, the one beginning at the top left hand corner.

Step 3—Ready mixed intonaco is laid on the wetted table and a small portion is made into a fairly wet skimcoat.

Step 4—The finishing trowel and the hawk is dipped in water and the skimcoat is laid as usual and floated with a small shingle float. Allow 15-20 minutes for setting, then carefully apply a spray of water to refresh the skimcoat and the finish of the intonaco can begin.

Step 5—Left over skimcoating is removed from the table and stored away. The tools are rinsed off and the rest of the intonaco lightly remixed and quickly and evenly spread out and troweled down to a thickness of approximately 3/16ths of an inch.

If the smooth intonaco has been decided upon, immediate troweling must follow quickly until the desired degree of smoothness is reached. If, on the other hand, a slight tooth is favored, floating with a smooth shingle float will suffice. Any additional finish over the floated surface with the trowel is inadvisable as it might result in uneven suction of the intonaco.

Step 6—If the intonaco is hardened enough to take a slight pressure of the finger, pouncing can begin and the first pounce is put in place, plumbed and dusted off or imprinted on the intonaco. Identical work is done in the piecemeal plastering whether sand or marble dust intonaco has been used.

SURFACING THE INTONACO

An attempt to reach the highest degree of smoothness on a fresco surface is neither necessary nor desirable. Large areas or panels cannot be troweled to an allover finish of uniform exactness because of the plastering in piecemeal fashion and the atmospheric changes from day to day. Panels with 4 to 6 painting parts should not be particularly hard to work up to a high degree of finishing but it will be almost impossible to keep uniform larger areas with numerous joints. Prolonged or sustained troweling will produce a fine network of lace-like cracks further pronounced by the color coat.

In connection with other finishes in the interior to be decorated, the semi-gloss finish of the fresco will add to the general effect, especially in murals of a purely decorative character.

In pictorial murals, intended to be seen from many directions in a large room, too fine surfacing takes away much of the strength and the effectiveness which are the true characteristics of the fresco mural.

It has been demonstrated in the most forceful manner

throughout the years of the author's experience that the floated lime-sand finish is the strongest and least sensitive to injury from outside causes.

Once, in a burning building, the hot walls, some unfinished and some finished in secco painting, were sprayed with the fire hose yet were uninjured except for streaks of smoke and dirty water. The breaking of a few inches off the top was caused by the ceiling falling in! The only crack was one in the corner of a partition wall of weaker construction. The painted walls had the streaks removed and the colors retouched none the worse for the experience. From the other walls the soot was brushed off and refinished with a thinner coating floated over the old one.

Lime mixed colors painted over floated lime-sand intonaco probably produces the most durable of all fresco surfaces.

COLORS

The fresco palette of today is usually made up from manufactured colors that will ultimately undergo many changes and have many new colors added from time to time such as the COAL TAR COLORS. These however belong to the group of entirely transparent colors and have only a limited function in fresco painting. Some of the colors are claimed to be limeproof but only time will prove this assertion.

MADDER LAKES are also recommended as lime proof and suitable for the fresco painter although none of them are known to be foolproof in lime. An overdose of tones made from them or the coal tar colors will also throw the color scheme into a confectionery sweetness wholly alien to fresco.

ALIZARIN MADDER can be tolerated in secco painting in very dark color schemes where reds, red-browns and blacks are used in profusion and where a glaze over an otherwise dull and uninteresting tone will give it depth and richness, provided it is not used over or mixed with Vert Emeraude or iron oxides.

VERT EMERAUDE

In selecting dependable colors for use in fresco-painting the reliability of the color man or manufacturer must be considered. Through experience the author has come to the conclusion that hardly more than half a dozen old reliable colorhouses have specialized in fresco pigments and from each one only certain shades were selected for their outstanding qualities. For instance, deep cobalt blue was acquired from one house, while from another came the beautiful ochres and from a third the mars colors or certain greens. Buying dry colors is quite different from buying tube colors for the latter should, if possible, come from the same manufacturer for the sake of both quality and uniformity.

LIST OF PIGMENTS FOR FRESCO PAINTING

White

Milk of lime
Blanc fixe
(Sulphate of Barium of limited use only)

Orange

Cadmium orange

Green

Vert émeraude
Oxide of chromium opaque
Green earth (Terra verde)
Veronese Green Earth

Red

Cadmium red, deep
Cadmium red, brilliant
Light red (English red) pure

Venetian red
Caput mortuum, light and dark
Terra rossa
Terra di Treviso
Terra Pozzuoli
Burnt Ocher, pure

Brown

Brown ocher
Burnt Sienna, deep
Raw umber, greenish
Burnt umber
Burnt green earth

Yellow

Cadmium yellow, medium
Cadmium yellow, deep
Yellow ocher

Golden ocher	*Blue*
Dark ocher	Cobalt blue, deep
Mars yellow	Cerulean blue
Naples yellow, lt. and dk.	Ultramarine blue, Guimets.

Violet	*Black*
Mars violet	Ivory black
Ultramarine red	Vine black
Ultramarine violet	Charcoal black

The colors on the above list are the so-called NORMAL SERIES OF FRESCO COLORS. Many of them have been known since the beginning of fresco painting and the others have a long standing reputation as reliable pigments. Several have been omitted from the list because of poor setting quality, others for their inclination to darken and bleed through super imposed tones and a few because they are exceedingly hard to mix with water.

Even with the shortcomings in violet and black pigments, the present palette should hold enough possibilities for any fresco work. Lime proof violet colors are few and not of a true violet shade, ie: MARS VIOLET, ULTRAMARINE RED and ULTRAMARINE VIOLET. Mars violet of a somewhat heavy color tone is perfectly reliable and sets well in lime. In heavily painted layers, however, the great opacity of the pigment tends to overpower bordering color areas. In glazings, the color acts as a binder over other colors. ULTRAMARINE RED and VIOLET are of limited use and then only indoors. The same can be said of ULTRAMARINE BLUE. Outdoors they are easily attacked by polluted air and the same may happen indoors, although slowly, where large gatherings of people are frequent and proper air conditioning is lacking. In some of the older theatres the author has seen ultramarine blue with whitish spots and brownish streaks from just such causes.

COBALT VIOLET (cobaltous phosphate) is not a good fresco pigment because of its bad setting qualities. Part of the pigment will set in lime only to rub off when dried out. Applied in a good binder it can be employed in secco painting. Cobalt violet of the cobaltous oxide arsenate type is very poisonous in powder form and should be handled with care. It is however not a fresco color.

Of the blacks, the IVORY BLACK, VINE BLACK, and CHARCOAL BLACK are all true fresco pigments. Carefully painted out, they hold and set in lime without rubbing off. In painting sequence, they must come among the first to be painted because of the slow setting. All such colors must have the first choice of the intonaco surface. Overlaid tones of other colors act as binders for the poorer setters but only in the top layers. Blacks will sometimes give better service when arranged into cold and warm tones as in the following examples:—A mixture of vine black and ultramarine red or violet makes a COLD BLACK while ivory black with vert emeraude or green earth serves as a WARM BLACK.

Tonality standards such as the two mentioned will quickly indicate the tone value in fresco, where limited time does not allow lengthy working up of the values.

As a neutralizing silvery GREY, charcoal black mixed with lime-white, lends itself in a beneficial and quieting way and helps reduce loud and unruly color schemes. Many uses will be found for it also as a passage or middle tone.

Another pigment, playing the same role in colorful paintings bordering on the gaudy, is the BURNT SIENNA. A small patch, sometimes only an indication of the tone will bring order and peace to the boldest of color riots. Investigation will prove this a fact. Cobalt blue with deep burnt sienna gives tones a depth clear in color whereas ultramarine blue would make only a sooty grey.

RAW UMBER, as a color factor, has little value in fresco and functions only as an occasional glaze over other colors and then as a binding agent. Heavy overlays of the color appear sooty and turbid.

BURNT UMBER and BURNT GREEN EARTH are superfluous in fresco painting. The former sets poorly and is apt to deaden an otherwise brilliant array of tones. The opposite can be said about the OCHERS, RAW OR BURNT. They are the ideal and perfect fresco pigments. In mixtures, they leave clear and well defined tones, work well with other colors and have a beneficial influence upon their setting. Of course this applies only to the genuine and unadulterated ochers. Tests for impurities, such as humus or "improvements" with coal-tar colors, are made by heating over a flame. True ochers turn red whereas presence of organic matter will turn the test sample black. Discoloration in alcohol is but further evidence of adulteration or a pigment not thoroughly washed nor entirely free from impurities. Red ochers frequently have a filler ground in to add to the weight. When shaken in a glass of water, the colors will divulge many secrets of adulteration.

Well washed RED EARTHS like the TERRA ROSSA AND TERRA DI TREVISO, of ancient reputation, are valued in fresco for their cool beautiful tones and their permanence.

TERRA DI POZZUOLI is another old fresco color. It is a natural cement and sets rapidly, before all other colors, thus hindering the adhesion when painted over with other pigments. Stress should therefore be laid upon the sequence of its use, that is, it should be painted lastly rather than among the earliest of the pigments and only in overpainting and not as a under-painting color. In spite of this characteristic its usefulness in fresco is well established.

Of the artificial iron oxides, the MARS YELLOW and MARS VIOLET are among the strongest. They have a good reputation in lime painting, in mixtures with other colors and are of very good setting quality. MARS YELLOW has a deeper brilliance

55

than yellow ocher, is more transparent and makes a good contribution to the ochers.

But for its dense heaviness in conjunction with other color tones MARS VIOLET would have a wider use in fresco. Its usefulness is rather in light transparency than in dark values where it appears to be immovable.

The one reliable blue in fresco is COBALT BLUE DEEP; reliable in this case meaning also paintable or a good brush color. Very light shades are the lowest grades of the product and probably have been stretched out with a filler of one sort or another. Only the deep shade of this pigment should be acquired for fresco painting. Violets and greens are equally easy mixed from this blue as are the great varieties of blue tones, provided the painter will remember the old rule of cold under warm and superimpose the colors in this sequence.

It should be pointed out that only two colors are mixed together; the third is always used as an overlaid tone or as underpainting.

CERULEAN BLUE is a permanent pigment in lime painting. If used in fresco, it should be among the first colors to be painted because of its slow setting. It's tendency to powder off a little after drying can be prevented by the application of a light glaze of either earth green or vert emeraude, immediately after the setting has begun.

OXIDES OF CHROMIUM, opaque and transparent brilliant, and the well known VERT EMERAUDE are the most permanent of all fresco colors, if not in all other techniques. Both colors have endless varied uses in fresco, not only in landscape verdure but equally in colorful shadows. Where real depth in a transparent darkness is called for, vert emeraude will produce such an effect in conjunction with other colors and without a pronounced heaviness.

In ancient works of fresco painting the two colors GREEN EARTH (TERRA VERDE) and VERONESE GREEN EARTH are always present. From the beginning of fresco, neither of the colors have ever been really excluded from the fresco painter's palette. The warmer Green Earth and the lighter, cooler Veronese Green Earth are, when genuine and pure pigments, perfectly lime-proof and extremely useful. Much of their reputation comes from their use in flesh-shadow colors and half lights. In thin overpaintings they never lose their soft lightness and in lime-mixed tones they become silvery optic greys in perfect conformation to fresco painting.

For brilliancy and color strength, the CADMIUMS take first place among the fresco pigments. The fresco painter will however soon learn that for real strength in the fresco mural he must rely on the less alluring iron oxides.

Only deep shades of the YELLOW CADMIUM are permanent in fresco or at least do not show a perceptible change of tone.

CADMIUM RED DEEP and RED BRILLIANT, the shade of Chinese vermillion, are the only two necessary ones, the rest of the lengthy list of shades will only burden the palette and confuse the painter.

CADMIUM ORANGE and NAPLES YELLOW set slowly and poorly in lime painting. These shades can readily be mixed from other colors and the pigments in question excluded from the fresco palette.

The vexing problem of a paintable white in the fresco technique is still with us as in ancient times. Among the many and varied experiments the author has made with different pigments to produce a good fresco white, MILK OF LIME seems to be the only one NATURAL IN FRESCO. Anyone used to painting with gouache or glue colors (where a white filler works in much the same way as the lime) should be adept in the use of lime mixed colors.

The transparency of the lime is the one characteristic that makes it fairly difficult to get used to, in order to judge the final value of the tone before the color is completely dry. As the drying may take considerable time, the only way out of the dilemma for the painter is to acquire the experience by test painting on a movable panel and setting off samples on a lime painted porous brick. Time spent in this kind of painting exercise will have its reward in the final outcome of the mural.

Sulphate of Barium, BLANC FIXE has some merit as a white pigment, but cannot replace the milk of lime and must be tested thoroughly in painting samples before the product can be used.

Preparation of the Milk of Lime White

Cookie like cakes of lime putty are laid out on new wooden boards to bleach in the sun. For a week or more they are turned over occasionally until they become exceedingly hard and white. The cakes are pounded into small pieces and, with distilled water, they are ground on a grinding slab with a muller to the consistency of heavy cream.

MILK OF LIME MAKING
EQUIPMENT

 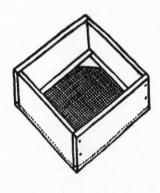

The equipment for making the MILK OF LIME consists of two one gallon stone crocks and a 56 mesh brass sieve of the same diameter as the top of the crocks. A long bristle brush is used to push the lime through the sieve and for cleaning purposes, a small sponge and a bucket of water.

Step 1—The ground lime is thinned in the first crock just enough to make it go through the sieve.

Step 2—The sieve is placed on top of the second crock and the lime is squeezed through until the crock is empty.

Step 3—The brush, sieve and crock are rinsed free from grit, the sponge applied over the sieve mesh until entirely cleaned.

Step 4—Repeat by again squeezing the lime through the sieve back into the first crock.

Step 5—Rinse the utensils as before and proceed in the same order making sure that all grit is cleaned off the sieve and the crock each time the lime is put through.

Step 6—Repeat as many times as possibles, at least ten, as milk of lime improves after each run through the sieve. It is essential to wash the sieve thoroughly after each use as the settling of lime in the mesh would soon spoil it and render the sieve useless.

Cellulose tape (pressed all around the edge of the frame, overlapping on the mesh about $\frac{1}{8}$", with another tape on the other side and the two tapes pressed together) will prevent the grit from accumulating on the edges and in the corners of the sieve. This tape is removed when the work is finished and the mesh thoroughly washed. A similar application of tape is used the next time the milk of lime is prepared.

PIGMENT TESTING

Each user of the fresco technique should take advantage of all the methods available that will contribute to a successful conclusion of the painting. Especially should time and attention be given to color testing. Two panels, one for making a color chart and the other for use in pigment testing, will enable the artist to familiarize himself with the materials and give him the necessary experience to assure a perfect result. Both panels should be made from the fresco ground. The color chart

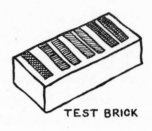

TEST BRICK

COLOR TESTING PANEL

should have each color painted a fresco in a square with the name of the color lettered above it for handy reference in color mixing.

For outdoor testing the colors are also set off in fresco painting, on either troweled or floated intonaco, in horizontal rows of vertical brushstrokes 1″ x 4″. Half of each color is covered with lightproof strips of oil painted plywood. After two or more months the strips are removed and the color samples examined. Any change of the pigment will show clearly and in case of failure of the color, it is removed from the intended palette. Test panels are of immense value to the work itself and should in no case be disregarded. By placing the panel out of doors to the full force of air, light, rain and sun, the reliability of the test is assured.

Further pigment testing by boiling in milk of lime is very simple. The pigment to be tested is mixed in less than a half coffee cup of milk of lime and a brush-stroke sample is set off on a lime-white painted dry brick. The rest of the color is poured into a test tube and boiled over a flame for about 10 or 15 minutes. After the boiling, the color is poured back into the glass and left to cool. The test tube is cleaned and the next unboiled samples are set off with inch intervals on the brick and the rest boiled as before. After a few samples have been boiled the first cooled color is set off next to its unboiled counterpart on the brick and by comparing the two, any deviation in shade can be detected. The strokes should be at least 3/4" wide to show a clear color shade.

COLOR GRINDING

Dry pigments for fresco painting are, as a rule, ground ready for use although a few manufacturers sell iron oxides in the rough. Rubbing the pigment against the thumbnail with the finger tip will reveal immediately whether or not grinding is necessary. Unnecessary grinding kills any color. In lime painting a slightly ground color is at its best and sets firmly but, if worn out by grinding, it dries to a lifeless greyish tone.

The GRINDING SLAB is made from a square piece of thick glass or a slab of hard marble. For a MULLER, any conveniently shaped piece of smooth hard marble will do, provided it is large enough to keep the fingers out of the color. A ready made

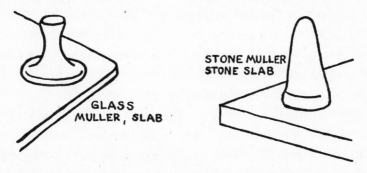

GLASS MULLER, SLAB

STONE MULLER
STONE SLAB

STONE MULLER may be procured from a lithographic supply house as well as a stone slab for grinding colors. Heavy slabs and mullers do the work twice as fast as smaller ones. A chemist's MORTAR AND PESTEL can be used with equal success. Test rubbing on the nail will tell when the pigment is ground to the desired fineness.

A small heap of the color to be ground is laid on the slab

61

MORTAR, PESTLE

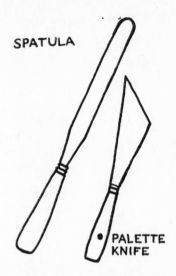

SPATULA

PALETTE KNIFE

and, with a long SPATULA or PALETTE KNIFE, mixed with distilled water into a paste. Little by little the paste is ground and only enough water is added to facilitate the grinding. Alcohol added, will help in colors hard to mix in water. The ground color is scooped up with the rinsed off palette knife and put into a labeled STORAGE JAR until ready for use. All fresco pigments are ground in distilled water to prevent them from getting mouldy in the closed jars. CANNING JARS with rubber rings and glass lids are ideal for wet storage of colors. The screwed on metal lids are unsatisfactory.

Dry pigments are kept in the well known waxed PAPER CONTAINERS for safe and dust proof storage. Every jar and container is provided with the proper label as to the name, mixture, etc. Glass jars, rubber rings and lids should be boiled before they are used to prevent mould forming on top of the colors.

BRUSHES

Painting over the tender moist intonaco requires long and soft brushes. At the beginning, when the intonaco surface is very sensitive, the first color tones are painted out with flat

62

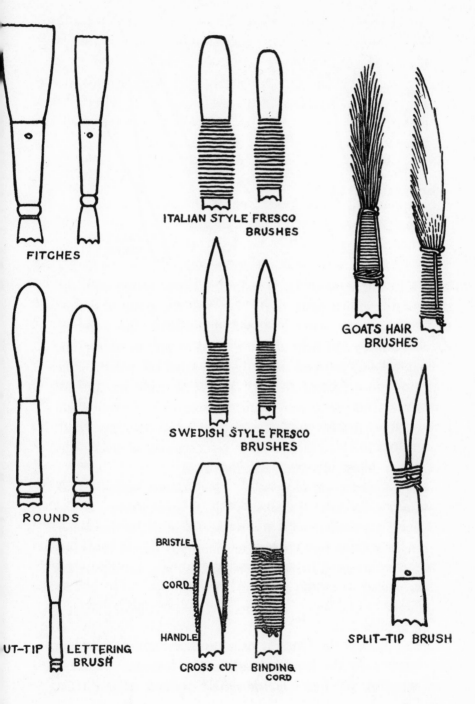

FITCHES

ITALIAN STYLE FRESCO
BRUSHES

GOATS HAIR
BRUSHES

ROUNDS

SWEDISH STYLE FRESCO
BRUSHES

SPLIT-TIP BRUSH

UT-TIP   LETTERING
BRUSH

BRISTLE

CORD

HANDLE

CROSS CUT   BINDING
CORD

63

broad SABLE BRUSHES. When this first coat of color has begun to set and harden a little, extra long BRISTLE BRUSHES can be employed.

The bristle brushes are made from pig's white and grey bristles. Grey bristle is used for the longest brushes, flat or round and without a point. White bristle is for the round and pointed.

All of the scenic painter's type brushes are used in fresco, the socalled FITCHES, CUTTERS, LINERS, etc., and are almost indispensable to the fresco painter. Sizes from 1/8" to 2" (round and flat), are the most practical ones. There are also bristle brushes made especially for fresco painting—the Italian and Swedish style, cordbound, FRESCO BRUSHES. The Italian brushes are usually made from long dark grey bristles and are stubby and without a point. The Swedish pointed are made from white bristles. Both kinds are important in lime painting because of their ability to hold a large amount of color. They are easily homemade, if the right kind of bristle is used. (See *illustrations*.) Fresco brush sizes run from 1/8" to 3/4". Still other types of brushes, for detail, lines and contours, are found among the china and pottery painting varieties and the CUT-TIP LETTERING BRUSHES.

For loose uneven color effects HOME MADE GOATS HAIR BRUSHES are especially adapted leaving streaky uneven brush strokes quite interesting as accents in the painting.

For certain looseness in surface treatments, the old fashioned marble imitators SPLIT-POINT brush is very useful. Such brushes were used in old dutch painting for making leaves on trees and masses of foliage. Later, they were adapted by the scenic painter for the same purpose. The author recalls having seen an antique "tjafser" (the Swedish name for this brush type) 5" in diameter and with as many as 8 points.

To make a split-point brush for fresco a strong white linen sewing thread is run in the bristle or sable, thus dividing it

64

into two points. Round brushes can be divided cross wise into several, flat ones in 2 or 3 places, according to the desired effect. The painters of old, by dipping the points in different shades, produced effects of charming naivité.

CUT SPONGES

Small soft toilette or face SPONGES of an even texture, can be utilized in many ways in the fresco technique. In their natural shape or cut, they can be used as brushes with a little practise. Smaller ones are held in a charcoal holder.

PALETTES for lime painting are selected from white, cheap, light CHINA PLATES or ENAMEL PLATES. Because of the lime, the colors will adhere in such a way as to make it impossible to wash them clean so the plate is discarded for a new one and because of this are more practical than the metal palettes with hollows or compartments for the colors.

COLORPOTS are selected for their ability to stand upright on scaffolding planks. STONE CROCKS, broad based COFFEE CUPS and low wide TUMBLERS all belong to that category of color pots.

The modern ELASTIC COVERS, in all sizes used for food protection, are perfect for keeping the colors dust free and for preventing the carbonization of lime mixed shades.

Tools such as a small HAND SPRAYER made of brass, a trowel shaped PALETTE KNIFE, a shiny flexible POINTING TROWEL (used for the purpose of giving depth to colors by troweling and enhance setting of difficult dark colors) WOODEN BUCKETS, GALVANIZED BUCKETS, pieces of TILE (for lifting out carbonized lime crystals floating on lime and lime mixed colors) are all parts of the painting equipment and are important to the final result, the mural. Small FUNNELS, made from oiled paper or cellophane, are very convenient (tied to the brush handles to keep the colors from running over the hand) a HAND REST, made from a slender bamboo pole, padded at one end to keep it from slipping when rested on the plaster surface outside of the intonaco, a WETTING BRUSH, a house painter's wall brush 4-5" wide completes the equipment for painting the fresco.

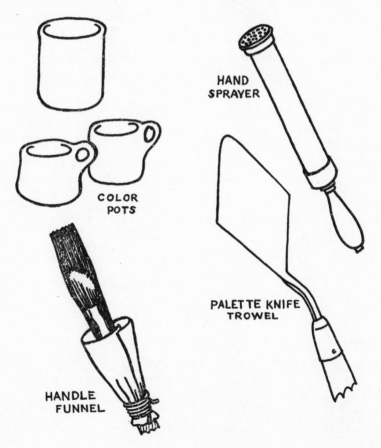

HAND
SPRAYER

COLOR
POTS

HANDLE
FUNNEL

PALETTE KNIFE
TROWEL

PAINTING THE FRESCO

CHAPTER EIGHT

THE FRESCO technique is similar to painting in tempera, gouache or water colors, in fact to all three combined.

Painters accustomed to any one or all of these methods will have little difficulty in the transition to fresco painting.

If the painter will keep in mind that fresco is something entirely apart from painting in oil (which may be done at leisure and without a time limit) and direct his effort towards simplicity in his design and color, then only will his work in fresco be of monumental mural quality.

The descriptive painting of a head (see *illustrations on pages 80 and 81*) should serve as a guide or an example of the sequence generally followed in superimposing the color tones making up the light and shadow; heightening and deepening of the colors, setting in reflected light and the completion of the painting in detail.

This description is the immediate follow-up of the previous description of plastering the first part of the intonaco in readiness for the painting. This should begin within the ½ hour allowed for the surface moisture to draw back or as soon as the pouncing of the drawing can be done.

Only by methodical superimposing of the tones in developing form in fresco, be it human anatomy, architecture or drapery, is it possible to keep under control what would otherwise easily end in confusion.

The two illustrations show a head painted in fresco technique, one developed only up to a certain point and the other fully completed.

As already indicated, the two examples are not to be looked upon as recipes for painting, only as illustrative help in clarifying the laying on of the different color tones in sequence and position to enhance the effect of the tonality.

The painting was developed from a pencil drawing on tracing paper, without the aid of a color sketch. Two twelve year old hard panels 18″ x 18″ were used for the painting. A thin skim coat was floated and the lime skin of the old sand finish consequently cut establishing a firm bond between the old and the new surfaces. This coating was left to dry until the next day, then an additional skimcoat without floating was laid.

Immediately over this second coat the full thickness of the intonaco was spread, about ⅛″ and troweled smooth to a fine finish. The three coats measured together less than ¼″. A twenty minute pause for preliminary work followed after which the underpainting took place.

The palette used in the painting was made up of the following pigments:—Yellow ocher, brown ocher, cadmium yellow medium, cadmium red brilliant, cadmium red deep, Venetian red, burnt Sienna deep, Cobalt blue deep, vert emeraude deep, terra verde and ivory black.

No lime white was used and the colors were mixed in water and painted out transparently.

THE PAINTING SEQUENCE

Step 1—After imprinting the drawing on the intonaco with a soft pencil run over the drawn lines, underpainting in terra verde was carried out in flat modeling, except over high lights and the lightest part of the local color.

Step 2—The shadow, made of brown ocher and Venetian red, was at first laid flat to avoid overmodeling.

Step 3—Cobalt blue and brown ocher were mixed into a passage tone, laid close to the edge of the shadow and slipping over in a couple of places.

Step 4—The local light was mixed from yellow ocher and Venetian red fluidly painted without modeling in the open space reserved for the light.

Step 5—The deep shadow was painted with a tone mixed from vert emeraude and the cadmium red, deepest shade, varied with burnt Sienna deep. The depth of this color depends upon the depth of the cadmium red. The author used a red bordering on purple.

Step 6—The ears and the lips were laid over with cadmium reds (brilliant and deepest). Over the terra verde underpainting, the eyes were finished in burnt Sienna and a little cobalt blue, completed with outlining in the deepest shadow color. This color was also used in the nostrils and the shadow on the shirt collar to the left of the cheek.

Step 7—Further modeling in the shadow was repeated as in Step 2.

To give the color tones time for setting and to allow the moisture to draw back from the surface, the background was underpainted in ivory black grey and the shadows in the shirt in a warmer grey with yellow ocher added. The same color was also used in the underpainting of the hair.

With the completion of the 7th step the painting had been developed as far as shown in unfinished state. (*See illustration.*)

In finishing the head it was first given an all over glaze, except for the eyes. The glaze was mixed from cadmium red, brilliant, and yellow ocher painted out with a flat broad sable brush of the showcard type.

Light strokes of vert emeraude, completed with Cobalt blue, broken with a little cadmium red deep, finished the background. The shirt was also finished with the painting of the shadow and the local light and detail set in fairly loosely in character with the deepest shadow color.

The finishing of the hair, with emphasis on the shadow, was made over a light overtone of the background color.

Attention was next given to the reflected light. From cadmium red brilliant and cadmium yellow, reflected light was painted over the shadow and on the edge and the back of shirt color in semi-transparent tones.

A light transparent overlay of the vert emeraude and Venetian red over the shadow on the nose and the cheek, deepened in hatching as in Step 5, completed the shadow.

Details such as eyebrows, depth in the hair, nostrils, deep hollows, etc., were also made with the deepest shadow color, with same variations of warmth with burnt Sienna.

The head was completed with a final wash of a light glaze made of yellow ocher and cadmium red brilliant, a lighter repetition of the first glaze after Step 7.

Such final glazes will help the setting of all colors and bring about an even distribution of overall color of the painting by drawing together the tones.

In most cases, only a wash with pure water will do because of the presence of small amounts of surplus color powders on the surface. These small quantities of color, if washed and distributed evenly, can in many cases do the work as well as a glaze. Washing or glazing should, however, only be carried out at the last moment when the colors are slowly starting to set and feel the pull of the ground. One must always be familiar with the setting ability and adhesive power of each individual color, to avert the disaster of lost colors. Abuse of glazes is another near disaster, as can be seen in works in fresco of the Italian renaissance.

The painting of the head was finished in 5 hours, including the making up of the tones, plastering, periods of rest and intervals of waiting for setting of the superimposed colors.

The colors used in the seven steps of painting were made up in pots for repeated use. Additional painting and finishing was done from an enamel plate palette.

Throughout the painting the following types of brushes were used:—No. 3 and No. 9 sable water color brushes, a cut tip lettering brush, two flat fitches ¼" and ¾" wide and a 1" wide showcard sable brush.

PAINTING WITH MILK OF LIME MIXED COLORS

Painting with colors mixed with milk of lime white is very much the same as true gouache painting or painting with the scenic painters glue and whiting mixed colors. The greatest difference is the transparency of the lime, which will make an accurate judgement of the dried shade a little more difficult.

The mixing of the big tones beforehand and the painting out of the test samples on a lime covered brick are the first preliminary steps taken before the painting can begin. All such pre-mixed tones are the leading colors throughout the painting and are mixed in labeled pots ready for repeated use. It should be pointed out that the quantity of each color must hold out to the end of the work. The original test samples are saved for any eventualities. Many an upset color pot has wrought havoc to a program of painting. The pre-mixed tones should of course be narrowed down to only the few that will be in repeated use, for instance shadows, local colors, etc. Heightening and strengthening, detail and drawing with the brush are all painted from the palette using the milk of lime white or the pre-mixed tones in combination with the ground paste colors on the palette. Mixing of more than two colors at a time is to be avoided here just as in any other color technique.

The experienced painter paints his lime mixed colors wet in wet as much and as quickly as possible. With the help of large fitches and fresco brushes, he aims at as nearly completed work as possible, leaving only detail and accents to be set in at the end of the painting and with the smaller brushes.

In such manner of execution and accomplished handling of lime mixed colors, paintings of great strength, force, and of true fresco character result.

By using forms in color, painted with less lime or transparently, fine effects in contrast can be achieved. Sharp accents in heavy lime-loaded color, near white and, set in where they will do most good, are brilliantly effective and should not be overlooked by the fresco painter. Fresco will only lend itself fully to painters with daring and courage, fully prepared to match their knowledge of painting with a vigorous material.

Toning down of too glaring values with a wash of glazing color is sound as long as it is done before any noticeable setting has taken place and then only as a straight even coat without brushmarking of unnecessary effect. In all such toning the character of the original vigorous brush work must be preserved and not lost in a weak looking over painting. In experienced painting with lime mixed colors the feeling of soft airiness with strength in tone follows after the drying. Quite impervious to surface injury, they surpass all other lime techniques.

Sometimes troweling with a flexible pointing trowel, especially over dark shadows will give depth and lustre to such worked over areas. Troweling over color surfaces should however be carried out when one is certain of the condition of the intonaco. Troweling over too fresh a surface might produce a grey film. The trowel is dipped in clean water or at times wiped dry before using.

Another method is rolling with a METAL ROLLER. A roller is made from brass or bronze about $1\frac{1}{2}''$ in diameter, 6 to 8" long, sloping slightly at each end and provided with a handle and rounded off edges. Depth in the color, obtained by pressing back with this roller is similar to the ancient practice of rolling a wine bottle over the painting, particularly over the faces, to give them smoothness and lustre. In dark colors additional painting may be done and a second troweling or rolling carried out. CELLOPHANE or CELLULOID support is used under the roller to keep it from pressing into the intonaco. Overdone troweling or rolling is worse than none at all. Very light troweling with a wet finishing trowel will also help to deepen the color shades but the handling of this trowel over finished work is more dangerous.

METAL ROLLER.

In summing up, this should be remembered, that the first two colorcoats serve as a means of conditioning the surface for painting and the true effectiveness of the colors is reached only after a certain amount of pigments have covered the intonaco surface and the pull is felt from it. In other words, when the foundation of underpainting is laid it helps in building up the overlayers exactly as the various mortar coats in plastering.

At the end of the work, the ideal condition of the color surface is reached and the culmination of that effect, lasting only a little more than an hour, will soon disappear. At this stage of painting, all finishing must be done and all accents set in because when this moment has passed, further work on the painting is impossible.

The experienced painter knows that in this equilibrium of the intonaco everything added seems to fall in perfectly, automatically and with ease. Therefore he will take good care not to overlook this possibility of a perfect finish to the day's work.

During hot summer days, the arrival of this moment of perfect balance comes early in the day. To keep it from coming too soon, a wet SHEET is hung overhead like an awning and is kept wet during the painting session and during short rest periods. Hanging a wet sheet directly over the painting, without touching the colors, will also delay the setting a little longer.

The painting of the color coats should be done in such a way that the color areas meet and blend without leaving small openings or partly covered brush marks. Such uncovered spots, spread all over the painting, will, in the final drying and bleaching of the lime, become exceedingly annoying and worse, will be almost impossible to retouch because of their number and minuteness.

Underpainting first transparently and ending in opaqueness is good practice and technically sound. On the other hand, glaze over opaque requires much care to prevent too deep setting of the underlayers before the glaze is applied.

Some painters are in the habit of drawing helplines, contours or markings directly on the ground with color, reasoning that color mixed with water alone will not make much difference under the intonaco. What actually happens, sometimes can be seen on old fresco-murals where the plaster has loosened and fallen over just such places where painting has been carried out over the ground mortar.

Plain water on dry lime-sand surfaces will set a spot hard if it remains there for any length of time. Some of the pigments will do that much faster and prevent overlaid mortar from adhering.

Charcoal drawing and snapped lines in charcoal are the only pre-drawn outlining that should be allowed on the ground. Before the plastering of the skimcoat, all such lines should have at least part of the surplus coal dust removed by slapping with a flexible straightedge, thus leaving only faint lines.

74

Another precaution worth remembering is to avoid pressing one's bare hands on the intonaco or, as is sometimes recommended, to blend the colors with the fingers. The author once saw a greyish print of four fingertips on the surface of a well known painter's fresco that had to be removed and retouched. The reason for this accident was probably hand perspiration.

JOINING

Next to perfection in painting, mastering the art of making a perfect intonaco joining should be the fresco painter's goal.

The unforeseen absence of the plasterers would seriously handicap the painter and he should therefore be eager to learn to do his own intonaco work in the event of such an emergency. This experience can best be obtained by practising on a test panel.

METHOD OF CUTTING THE INTONACO JOINING EDGE

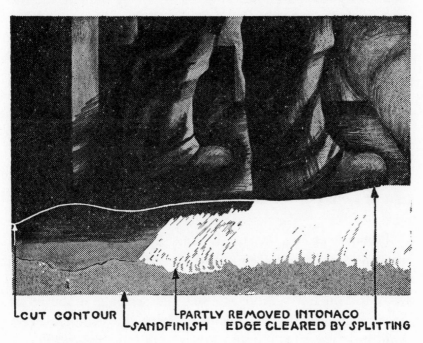

CUT CONTOUR   SANDFINISH   PARTLY REMOVED INTONACO   EDGE CLEARED BY SPLITTING

An important preliminary to the joining of the intonaco is the floating of a skimcoat over the dry and hardened sand finish. Such a coating has a two fold purpose, first to cut the hard lime skin on the sand finish and provide a good bond between the old and the new plaster coats, second to gradually build up the intonaco and at the same time hold the moisture as long as possible. Such moist mortar layers are of immense help in intonaco joining and prolong the time for the plasterers to do the work properly.

The cutting of the edge of the finished part to provide for the plaster joint contour, is done before the painting is finished or while it is still possible to cut into soft intonaco. The contour should have a curvature as simple as possible (without wedge like corners which are hard to plaster in joining), and should be done with a knife-like tool edge, pressed straight down to the hard floated surface and drawn along the contemplated contour. By following folds in garments, or by running the cut line into dark shadows, matching of the color will be simplified and invisible. To follow only the outlines of forms will bring them out in stereotyped silhouette with the color matching plainly visible. (See *illustration*.)

The removal of the intonaco margin outside the cut contour, is delayed as long as possible but must be done while the intonaco can still be split off without injury to the sharp edge of the contour. Also the margins should be left to prevent the moisture from leaving the outside edges too soon, with consequent setting of the intonaco and shortening of the painting time.

Removal of this margin is done by scraping the plaster coat down to the floated skimcoat. This must be carefully done and in such a way that the scrapings do not fly around and settle on the painting above. The scraping is started at the outside and stopped about 2" from the contour. From there the plaster coat is split off by pressing the square edge of the tool straight down. Piece by piece, it is split off until the clean edge of the contour is reached. This cleaning of the surface should not go beyond the skimcoat or the sand finish and the edge should be cut straight down, not slanting.

The surface is now ready to receive another part of intonaco and in the following step by step description the joining is fully explained.

The joining is made with the finishing trowel. Only small parts and tight corners are laid with the smaller pointing trowel. The laying of the joint as well as the troweling of the whole area, are continuous operations, therefore the reason for using the finishing trowel alone is obvious.

Step 1—The floated skimcoating is wetted down by painting water over the surface with a wall brush of suitable size. For the wetting of the cut edge a smaller brush is utilized to avoid splashing or slipping over the edge. A spot made in such a mishap is promptly lifted from the color surface by using a clean brush squeezed out in clean water.

Step 2—A watery skimcoat is laid thinly over the marked off painting part leaving a 6″ margin beyond the intended painting area.

Step 3—Immediately following the skimcoat, intonaco is quickly spread along the cut edge of the painted area and squeezed tight against the edge using the corner of the trowel. Intonaco squeezed over the edge is quickly folded back and accidental spots lifted as in step 1. The spreading of the intonaco and the troweling to an even thickness is done simultaneously.

Step 4—Dipping the trowel in water and quickly finishing the joint along the edge of the color followed by light troweling over the whole area are the best means of preventing the annoying dryness of the edge next to the joint. Prolonged troweling will cause steel to be rubbed off the trowel and settle as grey smudges on the intonaco. This should be avoided as much as possible. Speed only can prevent this from happening.

Step 5—Shortly after the finished troweling, the surface is given a light spray of water which is left to penetrate before the transfer of the drawing is made, either by imprinting or dusting with the pounce bag.

The following pages of illustrations are works in fresco painting, where the various descriptions of the techniques involved in the building up of the ground and the actual painting made a practical application under Mr. Nordmark's direct supervision.

These two illustrations show a self portrait painted by the author in Fresco Technique; one developed only up to a certain point and the other fully completed. (For a complete step-by-step description, see Pages 67 to 71.)

The painting of this self portrait was finished in
five hours including the make-up of tones,
plastering and the waiting intervals allowed for
the setting of the superimposed colors.

"TRANSFER OF MAIL FROM LINER TO TUGBOAT" BY REGINALD MARSH

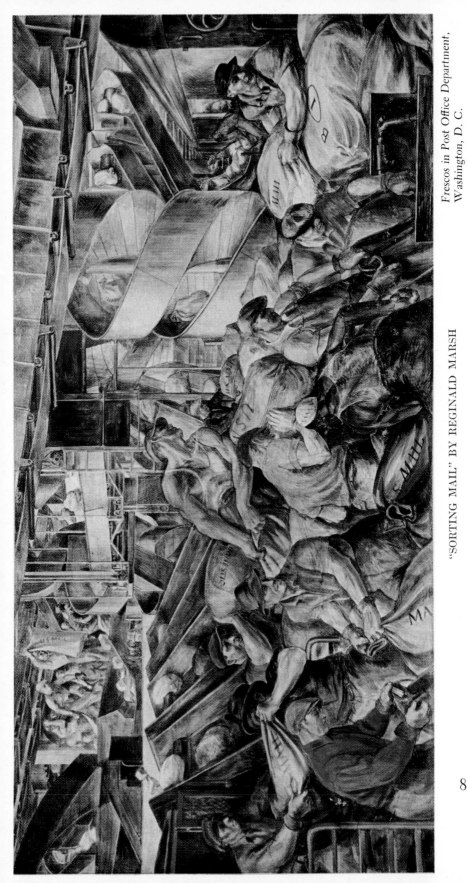

"SORTING MAIL" BY REGINALD MARSH

Frescos in Post Office Department,
Washington, D. C.

84

TVA WORKER AND FAMILY   PLEADING THE GOLD CASE

Four Fresco Panels by HENRY VARNUM POOR
Department of Justice Building, Washington, D. C.

CUSTOM HOUSE WORKERS   SURVEYING NEW LANDS

85

THE · SWEATSHOP · AND · TENEMENT
OF · YESTERDAY · CAN · BE · THE
ORDERED · WITH · JUSTICE · OF · TOMORROW

"SOCIETY FREED THROUGH JUSTICE" BY GEORGE BIDDLE

*Detail from Fresco in the Department of
Justice Building, Washington, D. C.*

SECCO PAINTING IN LIMECOLOR

P AINTING *in* SECCO should be of interest to many mural painters because of the ease of this technique. The painter, by using this method, can work more at leasure as the rigid time limit which confronts the fresco painter is eliminated.

The painting is done in combination with a LIME WASH over a well floated sand finished lime-sand plastering in the three regular coats, scratch coat, brown coat and sand finish.

TOOLS and MATERIELS are the same as those used in fresco painting. To the COLOR PIGMENTS listed as permanent in fresco a few more may be added, ie:—COBALT GREEN, dark and light, ALIZARIN MADDER, RAW UMBER, RAW SIENNA, MARS ORANGE and MARS BROWN. Some of the poorly setting colors (the blacks, blues and violets) if mixed in a weak casein binder can be used in the upper layers of the color tones.

The most important addition to the tools is a LIME WASH BRUSH. (See *illustration*.) This type of brush must be made from the highest quality 5" long grey bristle securely set in the handle. Only the best grades of such brushes will render satisfactory service in preparing the surface for successful secco painting.

Before proceeding with the step by step description of the preparation for actual painting, a few words should be said about the foundation color. Because of the necessity of underpainting in secco technique, the color tones of the lime-wash foundation become important to the tonality of the mural.

Painting over a pure white lime-wash is tedious and wholly impractical. Lime white bleaches and will, in time, bring out the color forms in a cold, hard and disconnected way. On the other hand a light colored surface tends to hold the color scheme together and lend support to the general impression of the tone as a whole.

LIME WASH BRUSH

The three following examples of foundation color have been used by the author and found very effective. For a warm whiteness, raw umber is well adapted to lime but only in light shadings, almost a silvery white. If made warmer with a small addition of yellow ocher, the tone takes on a slightly golden hue. A luminous neutral white, akin to the tone of the sand finish, is made by mixing ivory black, yellow ochre and light red in lime wash. Charcoal black in lime will render the wall silvery grey but of a somewhat colder tone.

The lime-wash is prepared as follows:

Step 1—Diluted putty lime is strained through a 29-32 mesh sieve into a steel drum holding enough lime to last throughout 6-7 coatings of the area to be painted. The first and second coats are made with white lime, without the foundation color.

Step 2—The respective colors to be used in the toning of

the lime white are separately stirred up in clear water, at first into a paste (to rid the colors of lumps), later diluted with water to facilitate easy mixing.

Step 3—Into the strained lime set apart for the last 2-3 coats, each color is stirred in one after the other through the strainer carefully checking the tone against a sample set off on a dry lime-painted brick. Pouring the colors through a strainer will keep them from streaking in the paint coat. A fine tea strainer will adequately serve the purpose.

Step 4—After the color tone has been reached, the work is begun by sweeping the sandfinish with a soft unused dusting brush to clear the surface of loose sand particles and dust.

Application of the Lime-Wash

Step 1—Clear water is sprayed or painted over the sand finish twice with a short interval to allow the first wetting to draw into the plaster coat. The second wetting saturates the surface.

Step 2—The lime-white is diluted with water to a transparent lime-wash and stirred until completely mixed. A few drops of the mixture on the thumbnail will indicate the degree of transparency when the first coat mixture is ready to use.

Step 3—The first coat is slowly and carefully painted out without leaving small uncovered spots, in secco a matter of importance. By dipping the brush only halfway into the wash and squeezing out the surplus paint against the bucket edge, the brush can be kept from dripping and running for a long time. The lime-wash is painted out in zig-zag strokes away from the face and without any marked direction and wet in wet keeping the paint edge from drying out too fast and from becoming a straight line. Curves and bulges on the edge will easily hide any joints apt to appear in the drying.

Step 4—Constant stirring of the lime-wash is imperative during the painting of the foundation if a well laid lime-wash is desired. Drying out of the first coating will be necessary to determine the condition of the lime-washing. A second slightly heavier mixture is painted out in the same manner, this time taking care to "even out" as much as possible. The third and fourth coatings are also made a little fatter by adding more lime or less water. The same principle is followed exactly as in plastering, fat over lean. All the coatings except the first are painted one over the other as the preceding one shows signs of drying.

Step 5—Immediately after the lime coats have dried to a fairly even whiteness, the color coats can be put on, painted as before. The stirring of the color between the brush dips is of the utmost importance to avoid a disturbing unevenness in the drying.

Step 6—The color coats are also made fatter by addition of less water or a heavier mixture. All the coats should be applied as carefully and evenly as possible. Direction of the brushing must not show and drowning of the characteristic grain in the floated finish should be avoided. The slight tooth in a floated surface holds the color film firmly and produces the sparkle and VIBRATO characteristic of lime painting whereas clogging of the grain by thick lime-wash, showing brush strokes, lowers the work to a painting over common white-wash.

If the mural is of very large proportions or a lengthy execution of the painting is contemplated, the last two coatings should be laid on in piece meal fashion to guard against too heavy carbonization of the lime-wash. Three to four day working areas can be covered ahead of time with the foundation color in one or two coatings before any appreciable lime skin will form. The foundation color in secco painting corresponds to the intonaco in fresco and only the lime used in fresco painting is usable in secco. All other kinds will come off as a white powder by rubbing and will cause endless trouble. Correction of such a mishap is possible only by re-plastering a new floated thin sand finish. Trials on the test panel will convince the painter that the warning is no exaggeration.

Only new and unused buckets and other utensils are in order for work in lime.

Just as in the preliminary work in fresco, the surface is inspected for cracks, spots, etc., which are repaired and the surface rendered fault free. A slight tooth left in the surfacing by the float will hold the colors indefinitely, especially if the work on the wall plastering has been carried out with the same care as in fresco plastering. Secco murals last as long as the constructed wall stands and is free from the danger of moisture seeping into the plaster, either through leaks or faulty insulation from the ground.

The preparation of sketches, cartoons and pounces is identical to that in fresco work. Colors and milk of lime are also made and stored as previously described. The same kind of brushes used in the same manner as in fresco are given an occasional rinsing in clear water during painting sessions and to prevent the colors from becoming diluted and weakened, the water is squeezed out of the bristles between the fingers after each rinsing. Pouncing charcoal dust is slapped off partly before outlining, finger marks and charcoal drawing is removed with the soft part of white bread, or in bad cases with a kneaded eraser.

Good practice in secco painting is given in the following step by step description and—just a reminder to the painter using this book—only good practice and plenty of it on a test panel will guarantee the outcome of the work.

SECCO PAINTING

Step 1—Outlining or brush drawing of the pounced drawing can be done with ivory black diluted to a grey or a weak yellow ochre, dark ochre or Mars yellow. Terra verde is also especially valued in preliminary drawing of this kind. The drawing is carried out with a few accents for the shadows to give a painted impression of the drawing rather than an outlined one. Too rigid outlining in a single running line tends to show through to the finish and a certain feeling of flat painting follows.

Step 2—Secco paintings have a peculiar characteristic of weakness before setting and hardening has taken place. Several months of setting might be necessary to bring out the full force of the painting since setting and hardening alone will give the final depth to the colors in all lime painting.

Through long experience, the author has found underpainting in light airy tones of a silvery quality to be the answer to the problem of keeping the color values at their full intensity. The underpainting will also help to keep the picture forms before the painter at all times and thus help him in the final evaluation of the tones in cold and warm contrasts as well as in the chiaroscuro.

Step 3—UNDERPAINTING in successive layers of yellow ochre, light red, terra verde and black is all mixed with milk of lime and used lean and fluid. Other colors such as Caput Mortuum and Venetian red are also employed in the underpainting usually in brighter spots of deeper coloring. Vine black mixed in milk of lime is used instead of a blue color and to give the under painting the much valued silvery tone so necessary for a clear value in the finished work. Strong colors must be excluded in the preliminary painting. Light variations in cold and warm and halftones, only slightly deeper than the foundation color are painted out in a flat fashion without any attempt at modeling. By painting over the outlined drawing in a free and loose fashion, the painter will not be bound to a given rigid style too early in the work. Each separate operation should give the impression of a finished work, the brush drawing as well as the underpainting. This impression, if maintained until the end, will be the best insurance for a perfectly balanced tonality.

Step 4—OVERPAINTING is done in colors mixed in LIME-WATER made by pouring 4 to 5 parts of water over 1 part of lime in a barrel. The lime is stirred up in the water occasionally to produce the lime water used in the mixing and diluting of all colors used for the work. Each time lime water is withdrawn, clear water is poured back and charged by stirring. As soon as the lime has settled down and the water has cleared it is again ready to be used. Carbonization of the lime floating on top of the water like ice floats is removed by lifting out with a dry piece of tile.

Step 5—The actual painting is done in transparent color at first and finished with milk of lime mixed colors, semi-transparent and opaque especially in the light shades. Some of the colors (blacks and blues) have a tendency to powder off by rubbing and should be prevented from loosening by adding a little fresh skim milk to the color. The formation of casein will prevent rubbing off of the top layers. 6 or 7 parts of cottage cheese mixed with 1 part of putty lime and diluted with 7 parts of water is a casein binder of ancient reputation. Such binders are however only used in the uppermost color coats and should be diluted to barely binding strength. Overdoses will give the color surface a greasy appearance.

Step 6—The sequence of the color tones follows the practice of laying warm over cold to preserve the clear transparency of the colors. Also never mix more than two colors together. The third is superimposed or under-painted. An occasional light brushing over the painted part with clear lime water is helpful, not only to set the under coloring, but immensely helpful in fine distribution of transparent overpainting.

Step 7—Erasure of secco paintings is best done by over-painting with lime white after the spot has been well wetted down. Several thin overpaintings with the lime are better than a couple of coatings with thick white which will pile up in very clumsy looking patches. The various coats should dry out before the next application otherwise the undercoating wil be unsatisfactory if the lime hasn't been given sufficient time to bite into the already carbonized undersurface.

Burnt sienna sometimes will bleed through such overpaintings with lime white. Even outlining with burnt sienna has sometimes worked through thin plaster coats. It is most important therefore to use the color in such a way that this characteristic will be the least harmful.

Painted out portions must be perfectly dry before any attempt is made to renew painting.

Step 8—Large color areas are always painted from pre-mixed colors in pots. In fact, most of the painting should be done in this same practical and speedy way.

Step 9—Murals within the reach of touching can be given extra protection by spraying with clear lime water several times, starting at the bottom and working upwards. Surplus color dust, washed off and in fine distribution over the painting helps to draw the tonality together and give distinction to the values. In case of disappearance or weakening of some part of the color, retouching with cheese casein mixed color will restore the painting.

MODELING OF RELIEF IN MORTAR

CHAPTER TEN

MODELING IN RELIEF of decorative elements in fresco or secco painting has been relied upon for special effects from ancient times.

Before the laying of the colors, all intonaco surface belonging to this part of the pouncing is carefully scratched and sharply defined in the painting.

Building up of the relief can only begin after the intonaco has hardened. Relief protruding more than ¾″ over the surface is reinforced by driving appropriate size COPPER NAILS into the scratched surface before the modeling takes place. Relief higher than 1½″ is built up with a scratched core over the nailheads made from a 1-2 sand-lime mixture with about 1/5 of the volume mixed with ATLAS STAINLESS WHITE CEMENT. As in the building up of a fresco ground, thorough moistening of each layer before the application of the next one must not be overlooked. Of equal importance is the occasional wetting of the cement coat for a couple of days before another layer is started.

Hammering in the nails before the intonaco has had sufficient time to dry hard, might jar it loose in the last plastered areas and should therefore be avoided at all cost. Only methodically carried out work in lime and sand will have any permanent value.

The pointing trowel and the hawk, together with a few steel MODELING TOOLS in various shapes, a small wetting brush and

95

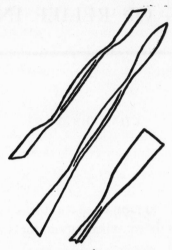

MOULDER'S TOOLS

a sponge is all that is needed for most of the work. The still fresh relief can, after the modeling is finished, be POLYCHROMED in fresco or after having dried out finished in wax gilding.

Relief up to 2″ can safely be modeled in mortar if sufficient care is taken in the building up of the core and time is given to let the intonaco dry and harden before any work is undertaken that might jeopardize the painting itself.

The painting can be safeguarded from dropping mortar by fastening profiles of the drawing cut from strong BROWN PAPER by following the pounced outlines. The pieces are fitted under each place where modeling is to begin and held in place with small squares of Scotch tape. If the painting has not dried sufficiently the Scotch tape will, on removal, peel off the color. Cellulose tape is too sticky and may injure the surface of the plaster.

GILDING

LAYING OF GOLD AND SILVER over parts of fresco or secco painting is generally left to a professional gilder. The painter should however be able to do the gilding himself. The method described below has been used by the author for many years and its simplicity of execution and permanence is very well known. The parts to be gilded, if not already marked in the painting, are outlined in white chalk either by hand or by pouncing.

YELLOW BEESWAX is melted slowly in a wax pot made from a narrow high tin can, provided with a wooden handle. (*See illustration.*) The heating can be done over an ALCOHOL LAMP or a STERNO DRY HEAT arrangement. A small alcohol lamp,

WAX POT WITH HANGING ALCOHOL LAMP

STERNO DRY HEAT ARRANGEMENT

attached to and hanging underneath the wax pot, is very practical for working overhead. Into the hot melted wax some VENETIAN TURPENTINE (of the very best grade obtainable) is poured. At first only a small portion, about a fifth, is poured in and a sample is tested for adhesiveness. The sample can be tried on any dry plastered surface and should have enough Venetian turpentine mixed with the wax to hold the GOLDLEAF securely to the wax surface. The wax should pile up from repeated overlayings in relief and should not break off after cooling and hardening. It must be used hot enough to flow out easily and leave a smooth surface. Repeated heating to keep it at flowing consistency is therefore of great importance

97

Overheating of the wax must be avoided because of danger of fire explosion and also because prolonged heating will spoil the Venetian turpentine.

VERMILLION RED mixed in the wax is used under goldleaf and ULTRAMARINE RED or some BLUE AND ROSE MADDER under genuine SILVERLEAF.

BRISTLE BRUSHES of different sizes are employed to paint out the wax medium. To prevent the wax from running over the hand, a small paper funnel is tied to the brush handle. To facilitate easier control of the hot wax in laying lines, lettering, etc., the brush handle is held tilted up, thus literally lifting the wax in place. This manner of handling the brush makes the wax run off quicker and out to the tip of the brush. Cooled and stiff wax is scraped off against the edge of the pot and remelted. Working overhead, the handle is held parallel with the surface to keep the wax from dripping.

By repeated over laying, the wax is easily piled up in relief and ornamentation in relief will set off the gold or silver against the painting strongly and effectively, in small scale on the color sketch as well as in full size on the mural.

Gilding or laying the gold leaf is simple. The GOLDBOOK is torn against the straightedge into strips of the same size as the parts waxed for gilding:—the width of lines, bands, letter staples, etc. Cutting with a pair of scissors will keep the gold from separating from the protective paper edge and tearing. The strip

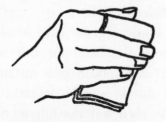

CORRECT HOLDING
AND MOVING OF THE
GOLDLEAF

is held inside the left hand between the index and middle fingers, folded back over the index finger and held with the thumb. One paper strip with a gold leaf is picked from underneath the thumb and, hanging outside the right hand, moved straight towards and laid over the wax and pressed down lightly, the paper cover is left to fall to the floor and before the gold is pressed home, the whole waxed part is laid piece by piece in the same way with the edges overlapping. A wad of surgical cotton is used to press the gold down firmly and a fluffy CAMEL's

GILDERS
DUSTER

HAIR BRUSH to dust off the surplus. If hundreds of books are laid, the loose gold is saved by holding a paper bag under the place to be dusted and together with the used cotton is sold to a dealer in old gold.

The laying of the wax should, if possible, be done only in warm temperatures as cold and dampness will make the wax harden and collect enough moisture on the surface to hinder the gold from adhering properly. Wiping with a soft rag will sometimes help to overcome the trouble, but working in a warm temperature will eliminate this altogether.

After a few days of drying and hardening, the gold or silver is rubbed off on the highlights with the hand. At first very little rubbing is done and the effect is judged from a distance, additional rubbing off or regilding can be done as desired.

Leaf protecting varnish, procured from a dealer in gold leaf, is applied over the gilding after the rubbing has been completed. This precaution is taken in places attended by many people such as churches and theatres. The protective varnish must be thin and invisible, especially made for the protection of gold leaf. Because of its rapid blackening by oxidation, silver should be protected as soon as it can withstand the brushing on of the varnish after hardening.

RETOUCHING

CHAPTER ELEVEN

Retouching in small patches on a new fresco or secco mural is quite possible if the painting is completely dry before the attempt to retouch is made.

Damp colors do not give the true shade and in as much as the retouching is done a secco, naturally the matching of tones must also be done against dry not damp colors.

Retouching if abused or carried out over a fairly large portion of the mural is next to worthless. Scraping off and replastering with new intonaco and repainting is the professional way of taking care of large size mistakes or weak painting in fresco. However, small patches or spots are frequently touched up by the painter and by a little experimentation on the test panel over a dry tryout painting he will soon find out how much he can touch up and still "get away with it."

SILICATE POTASH SOLUTION mixed with water, about 1 part of solution to 6 parts of water is, if experimented with a little, a good retouching medium. The colors are mixed in the medium in small quantities (for convenience in small color pots) and matched correctly with the original. Fresh medium must be made up several times during lengthy works as only with a perfectly fresh solution has the retoucher any guarantee of success.

On a test painting, small patches of the matched colors are painted out to determine, first, the strength of the medium to bind the colors and second, if when dried out the medium has the same sheen as the original so as to blend with the surrounding colors.

All color patching is done with small water color brushes, No. 7-9 or smaller. During the work with this solution, the brushes are frequently washed in clear water to keep the silicate from settling in the brush roots and, if left for a few minutes, they should be washed out before being laid down.

In the painting small brush strokes are laid side by side similar to the threads in rough woven material. By using small brushes, complete control of the color value is readily possible.

Color repairing on old murals is done in a slightly different manner. With pre-matched colors the spot is filled in with sloping lines. Seen in "close-up" the repair should be clearly noticeable, while from a distance it should blend with the surroundings and become invisible. In this way, no attempt has been made to hide the repair (important in work on valuable murals) and no appreciable change in tone will take place.

Retouching however is something to be avoided rather than to be relied upon as a possible margin of safety during the execution of fresco murals.

CLEANING

No attempt should be made to "clean" murals in fresco or secco painting without the help of an experienced technician. All cleaning should be of the least dangerous variety, DUSTING. A VACCUM CLEANER provided with a broad nozzle, without the brush, is one of the best tools for cleaning large murals by removing the dust, operation number one in all cleaning of works of art. Sometimes if a brush is used directly over the intonaco, sharp particles of sand, protruding over the surface, will catch in the bristles and break off leaving a white spot. RAGS will damage the surface in the same manner, when on the other hand a vacuum cleaner lifts the dust out without rubbing it into the myriad of small crevices present in plastered surfaces. To keep the edge of the nozzle from pushing off sand, it should be run over a piece of washed LINEN SCREEN about a yard square, stretched taut over a frame. The frame is held firmly over the surface in contact with the color film, thus acting as a protective surface over which to run the cleaner. The nozzle is run in all directions as straight running lanes would show after the dusting, particularly in artificial light.

Cleaning with water in spots is almost impossible on fresco and secco murals because of the settling of the dust on the surface and the danger of the greying of the colors after drying. This is especilly common when fine sand dust is present in the air. By dabbing a moist sponge on a dark color area, the firmness of the color film can be tested before water cleaning is attempted. Color coming off in such a test will not withstand any cleaning. Fixing of loose color can sometimes be done by spraying clear lime water over the spot. A FIXATIVE ATOMIZER with a fine spray is used and an interval of drying allowed between sprays. Two or three thicknesses of white blotting paper are held beneath the area sprayed to prevent the running water from streaking below.

On murals where all colors are found to adhere firmly to the intonaco and the plaster coat is free of faults, water cleaning can be done by using a hand sprayer and distilled water. The spraying is started at the bottom and continued horizontally upwards to enable the dust and dirt to run off on a wet surface thus preventing streaking and settling of the dirty water. Heavy white blotting paper is held in readiness to pick up surplus water and is used lightly and quickly to dry the surface superficially. In fairly old work this is a necessity as lengthy soaking might develop efflorescence caused by the presence of caustic lime activated by the moisture.

Piece meal cleaning takes skill and patience in any medium and to really know when a part can be called "clean" or has undergone some change in the cleaning process may sometimes "stump" even an expert.

The least dangerous and the well known methods in such undertakings should be tried first, before the wet mediums are resorted to. Erasure of soot and loose dirt with the soft inside part of WHITE or FRENCH BREAD, a day old, is fairly safe, provided the colors are holding firmly. As soon as the bread crumbs become dirty, they should be replaced with clean ones. Erasing is done in every direction to avoid visible straight lines and lanes. In spots where some color rubs off, the work should be stopped or done very lightly and shaded off into the nearest area already cleaned. Bread cleaning methods are old and well known in the removal of dirt from painted surfaces.

MODERN WALL PAPER CLEANERS of the eraser type, if guaranteed not to cause changes in the colors are other possibilities in cleaning murals. ART GUM or rubber erasers in general are dangerous to colors such as the ultramarines because of the sulphur film left after erasing and the abrasive quality of some of the harder kinds will eat into the protective film of carbonized lime.

Unwarranted cleaning and retouching is a bigger menace to paintings than a film of dirt or a spot of grease. In some cases the sad end of the entire painting tonality.

Maintenance of fresco and secco murals should be limited to a carefully carried out dusting every 15-20 years and filling in of color over repairs. All other cleanings and "improvements" are of very dubious value and actually dangerous to the painting if not done by or under supervision of an experienced renovator.

REPAIRING

Cracks, holes and deep scratches in fresco murals are, in general, not hard to repair. The same sequence used in the building up of the plastercoats, and the same mortar is also used in the repairing of damage or deficiency in the plaster coats.

Deep holes are thoroughly moistened with a small sponge to prevent the running of water over sound areas. The bottom of the hole is filled in with a 3-1 sand-lime mortar criss-crossed a little with the trowel point. The second filling is made from a 2-1 mortar and applied after some drying of the bottom filling. Good wetting of the mortar layers is essential in repair work as well as drying in between fillings. If sand intonaco has been used, a similar 7-5 intonaco is used, otherwise a 1-1 marble dust coat is sufficient.

Large patches are painted in full fresco from pre-matched colors, tested for true shades and values and made up in color pots, labeled with full information to avoid mistakes in the application. Small holes and cracks are moistened and soft fine intonaco is squeezed down. Mortar, squeezed out over the edge is lifted off with a palette knife while still fresh to prevent its adhering to the painted surface. Sometimes when ragged edges in cracks would prevent a clean job, it may be necessary to cut such edges clean without widening the crack. Smaller repairs are left to dry out and are touched up in silicate potash colors. At times the shape or the nature of the damage will prevent the mortar from penetrating into the

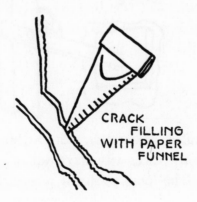

CRACK
FILLING
WITH PAPER
FUNNEL

crack, etc., in the proper way. Through the utilization of small PAPER FUNNELS in the same way as the bakers decorate their cakes, very neat repair jobs can be done with ease. Strong PARCHMENT PAPER, used in cooking, is especially useful for making the small funnels. They are held together with rubber cement and the opening cut to fit the place to be repaired. A fine mixture of marble dust intonaco, pushed through a sieve is used for filling up the crack. The mixture is poured into a funnel and after closing the top by folding the paper twice, the intonaco is pushed into the crack by squeezing the funnel as you would a paint tube. Soiling of the surface below the place of repair is prevented by covering with a piece of paper fastened with SCOTCH TAPE and the under edge of the paper bent up to catch falling intonaco. Moisture under the tape will prevent hard sticking and just briefly hold the paper to the color film.

Loose and bulging intonaco can, in some cases, if not too far out from the plaster base, be repaired by squeezing a prop-

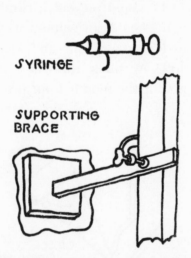

SYRINGE

SUPPORTING
BRACE

erly compounded CEMENTING AGENT through pinhole openings in the faulty places with a SYRINGE, a special kind of small hand sprayer. The loose plaster is pressed back slightly and a piece of FELT is laid over the repair and over this a piece of board, a little larger than the repaired place. The board is held in place by a support wedged in between the board and the scaffolding where it is left until the cement has dried and safely anchored the loose intonaco. The nature of the loose plaster coat and the age of the mural will determine the kind of cementing agent to be used. The syringe is also used in filling cracks and cementing flaking color surface.

PRELIMINARY WORK FOR PLASTERING

IN ORDER to prevent damage from lime plastering, extensive covering of floors, paneling, pilasters, pillars, statutary, etc., must be carried out. Hardwood floors, oak floors, finished or unfinished, are especially sensitive to lime. Wax is no guarantee against prolonged action of lime. The following system of floor covering has been worked out by the author and used with success to insure perfect safety for the interior finishes.

Lengthwise, over the wooden floor, lengths of BUILDING PAPER are laid out, after the floor has been swept free of dust and grit that might mar the finish. The edges must overlap 5" and have strips of strong BROWN PAPER pasted over the joints to prevent them from slipping and to prevent the grit from penetrating between. The paper is cut clean and tight against the baseboards.

Over this paper covering, heavy ROOFING PAPER is laid with 3"-4" overlapping edges placed between the underlying joints to secure a tight cover. The edges are left open without the pasted strips and the open edge faced away from the fresco so that the sweeping will be away from it also. Bricks or other weights are placed on the edges to keep the paper in place.

Along the baseboard, WOOD LATH strips are nailed over the paper, tight against the baseboard. Fine FINISHING NAILS are used leaving only insignificant holes that will fill in when the

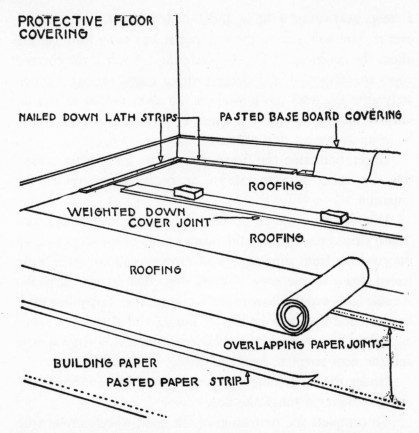

PROTECTIVE FLOOR
COVERING

NAILED DOWN LATH STRIPS   PASTED BASE BOARD COVERING

ROOFING

WEIGHTED DOWN
COVER JOINT

ROOFING

ROOFING

OVERLAPPING PAPER JOINTS

BUILDING PAPER
PASTED PAPER STRIP

floor is waxed. Strong PAPER strips are pasted on the edge of
the baseboard. These should hang loose and be wide enough
to cover the lath strips to prevent water from seeping under
the floor covering. Window glass is protected from being mortar
spattered by placing newspapers over them. Over large windows,
starting from the bottom, newspaper is hung, held in place
with small dabs of paste and overlapping in successive layers,
if necessary, to the top. The windows are uncovered when the
plastering is finished and covered again when a new coat is
about to be laid.

Wood paneling is covered by hanging paper over it and
pasting the edges to the edge of the wood next to the fresco
ground. The wood is completely covered and over the paper

109

a clean TARPAULIN is hung and fastened by lath strips nailed over it. This will prevent the wet mortar and water from getting under the covering. When the plastering is finished the covered edges are scraped off and cleaned with a WHISK BROOM immediately after the work has moved on. To allow mortar to stay on finished interior moulding or edges, even though covered, would be to invite a great deal of trouble.

Edges, bordering the fresco ground, are given extra protection by using WATERPROOFED or OILED paper under the tarpaulin.

Wooden stairways are covered in the same fashion as floors. A lath strip is nailed along the inside corner of the steps to keep the covering from slipping. As an extra precaution, boards are nailed down to the edge of each step. Boards over tarpaulin are also laid over the floor in the working area. Tarpaulins must be clean and free from holes and, during and after water spraying, all puddles should be quickly removed with a large sponge and the floor swept to facilitate drying.

Under the scaffolding uprights, a piece of new board will prevent chafing through the floor covering.

To complete the protection of the floor, wheelbarrows with rubber wheels should be run over plank runways and extra tarpaulin and planks placed under the mortar box.

Marble pilasters and mouldings, etc. are protected by pasting white newsprint over the surfaces and sculptured work and columns by additional boarding up. Marble floors are covered the same as wooden ones, except that instead of nailing strips, the boards are weighted down.

The paste used for applying the paper to the surfaces to be covered must be such that simple moistening with water will facilitate its removal. STARCH OR FLOUR PASTE is generally used and is made as follows: Either one is mixed with cold water and allowed to boil for a few minutes. The paste should not be too heavy and is ready for use when cold. The paper is laid out in rows with the edges overlapping ½". The paste is applied in one operation to all sheet edges with a 2"-3" brush. All work to safeguard the interior should be done with great care, while working with lime mortar and is of the utmost importance. Negligence in the use of lime and mortar, water spraying, brick cleaning with acids or the dropping of heavy tools or planks may cause irreparable damage to a finished interior. Accidents such as the kicking over of buckets or color pots or the dropping of color loaded brushes are among the most frequent ones.

Oak turns black from the action of the lime while anilin stains will bleach in spots from lime. Both are impossible to repair invisibly. The glossy finish of marble may turn mat and dull from lime-mortar spatter.

COLOR BOXES (see *illustration*) for keeping color pots, brushes and other tools are the best safeguards against such accidents.

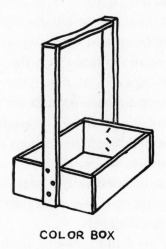

COLOR BOX

THE SCAFFOLD

THE PAINTER of an extensive mural usually inherits the scaffold from the plasterers and other workmen. If he is not experienced or accustomed to working on a scaffold, he should take a few extra precautions before taking over the uprights and braces, planks and a good deal of debris which will comprise his future working place.

His first task should be to have it cleaned up. Then the carpenters should reinforce it to eliminate the swaying always caused by its having been used for heavy work for some time. The planks should be straightened out, the warped ones either replaced or have wedges placed under the ends. Painters all have the habit of stepping back for a better view of the painting, therefore a waist high rail should be attached on the outside as the scaffold would be dangerous without it.

All walking planks must be of exactly the same thickness as any difference in thickness might cause a bad fall. Even a good scare caused by the sensation of falling off is a bad feature of planks of an uneven thickness.

To have a tight floor laid to walk on is unnecessary. Regular heavy unyielding scaffolding planks, free of big knots and laid out with 1¾" openings between them are adequate. They are easy to move to one side for a free unobstructed view through the scaffold from below when working high up on a wall or a ceiling. Before moving planks or reinforcing the scaffold, etc., the fresh part of the paintings as well as the color table must be covered to prevent settling of the dust which always arises during such work. If the scaffold is going to be used for a considerable length of time, the ends of the planks are generally nailed down to prevent them from slowly slipping out of place and causing an accident. Extra planks under the working tables on the scaffold prevent them from shaking and upsetting the color pots.

If improvements on the scaffold are needed it is best to have a carpenter do such work. When a large and complicated scaffold is used it becomes doubly important to be assisted by experienced workmen.

When walking planks are extended and laid end to end, they must be nailed down. If the plank ends are placed one above the other they should have small wedges placed under the raised plank ends to prevent wobbling.

Do not use stepladders on scaffolds, instead have a carpenter make up a few STEPS, wider than a stepladder and easy to move around. This arrangement is especially convenient when an extra scaffold would obstruct the view and take up valuable space.

Another practical hint is to place the water bucket on one single plank, not over the openings of two planks as stepping on either one will upset the bucket immediately or at least spill the water.

A PULLEY with a strong ROPE attached to an extending bar on the outside of the scaffold is a great help in hoisting up heavy materials.

Last, a water hose which reaches to the top and across is very convenient.

Instead of the light-blocking and shadow making heavy wooden scaffold of former days; the painter of today can have the enjoyment of working on the modern, slender locking steel scaffold made from steel tubing. Rigid and safe, with most of the bad features of the wooden scaffold eliminated. The modern scaffold seems to have endless combinations of practicability.

SOURCES OF SUPPLIES

O NLY the highly specialized materials and tools of the trade have been classified. Common building material such as bank-sand for the plastering trade can be found locally as a rule.

The quality of the pigments from the color houses and the lime from the listed firms is well known to the author from long experience.

Brushes and trowels should be purchased from manufacturers or supply houses specializing in such items.

BRUSHES

Cordbound fresco brushes, scenic painter's fitches, cutters, liners, sable water-color brushes, cut-tip lettering brushes.
Source: M. Grumbacher.
460 W. 34th St., New York, N. Y.

Scenic painter's fitches, cutters, liners, riggers.
Source: A. Leiser & Co.
48 Horatio St., New York, N. Y.

Water-color brushes, show-card, stripers, sky brushes, gilders, dusters.
Source: F. Weber Co.
1621 Chestnut St., Philadelphia, Pa.

CEMENT

Atlas White Stainless Cement.
Source: Building material dealers and lumber yards.

COLORS

Lime proof pigments for fresco and lime-secco painting.
Source: Fezandie and Sperrle Inc.
205 Fulton St., New York, N. Y.

M. Grumbacher (Schmincke fresco colors)
460 W. 34th St., New York, N. Y.

F. Weber Co.
1621 Chestnut St., Philadelphia, Pa.

Permanent Pigments
1127 Sixth St., Cincinnati, Ohio

Winsor & Newton Inc.
31 Union Square, New York, N. Y.

Schneider & Co., Inc. (Block powder colors)
123 W. 68th St., New York, N. Y.

COLOR GRINDING EQUIPMENT

Mullers, slabs, palette knives, spatulas.
Source: The Senefelder Co., Inc.
32-34 Greene St., New York, N. Y.

Glass mullers and glass slabs:
Source: Artist's supply stores.

DISTILLED WATER

Source: Water dealers, consult the classified telephone
book.

DRAWING, DETAIL, TRACING PAPER

Source: Arthur Brown & Bro.
67 W. 44th St., New York, N. Y.

Keuffel & Esser Co.
60 E. 42nd St., New York, N. Y.

FIBER

Cocoanut fiber, goat's hair (used in scratch coats).
Source: Building material dealers, lumber yards.

FURRING MATERIALS

Source: Building material dealers, lumber yards.

GOLD AND SILVER LEAF

Source: W. H. Kemp Co.
43 W. 16th St., New York, N. Y.

LIME

Aged high calcium lime putty in steel drums (9 cubic feet per drum).
Source: Colonial Sand & Stone Co., Inc.
30 Rockefeller Plaza, New York, N. Y.

Unslaked high calcium lime, powdered, in paper sacks and barrels.
Source: Veri-Fat powdered quick lime in 100 lb. sacks.
Ashgrove, Missouri Lime Co., Mo.

Peerless White Lime Company
Ste. Genevieve, Mo.

METAL ROLLERS

Source: Ordered from local machinists.

117

MIXING HOES

Source: Hardware stores.

MORTARS AND PESTLES

Source: Eimer & Amend
633-35 Greenwich St., New York, N. Y.
Drug stores

PERFORATING WHEELS

Source: Artists supply stores.

PLUMBLINES NON-TWIST, PLUMB BOBS

Source: Hardware Stores.

SAND

Source: Colonial Sand and Stone Co., Inc.
30 Rockefeller Plaza, New York, N. Y.

Banksand (river sand) No. 67 coarse, No. 66 fine.
Source: Whitehead Bros. Co.
537 W. 27th St., New York, N. Y.

Banksand (Cow Bay), coarse.
Source: Exner Sand & Gravel Corp.
880 Zerega Ave., The Bronx, New York, N. Y.

Quartz sand, fine and rough.
Source: Penn Glass Sand Corp.
Louiston, Pa.

George F. Pettinos
1200 Locust St., Philadelphia, Pa.

MARBLE MEAL AND MARBLE DUST

Source: Building material dealers.
In other localities consult the classified telephone directory or order through the local building material dealers or lumber yards.

SIFTING SCREEN MESH

Source: Patterson Bros.
15 Park Row, New York, N. Y.
or local dealers.

SNAPLINES

Source: Hardware stores

SPONGES

Small face sponges.
Source: Drugstores

Sponges for the trade.
Source: Painter's supply houses

SPRAYERS

Hand sprayers.
Source: Hardware stores

STRAIGHT EDGES

Beveled 45″ long.
Source: Tailor's supply houses

Plasterer's 6″ long, straight grained board ⅞″ x 6″.
Source: Lumber yards

SHINGLES SUITABLE FOR FLOATS

    Source: Lumber yards

TROWELS

"The Xtralite Finishing trowel" sizes 4x12 and 4x14 Browning trowels, pointing trowels, hawks, float handles.
    Source: Marshalltown Trowel Co.
    Marshalltown, Iowa
    Hardware stores

WATERLEVELS

    Source: Hardware stores

WATERPROOFING

            Toch Bros. RIW asphalt waterproofing and marine cement.
            Building materials supply or lumber yards.

WAX

Yellow beeswax.
    Source: Drugstores and chemists supply houses

VENETIAN TURPENTINE

    Source: H. Behlen and Bros.
    10 Christopher St., New York, N. Y.

    Eimer & Amend
    633-35 Greenwich St., New York, N. Y.

INDEX